MEDITATING AS A CHRISTIAN

For
Jeffrey N. Steenson
David P. Mills
and all catholic
Evangelicals and evangelical
Catholics who seek for
renewal in the
Episcopal Church, U.S.A.

PETER TOON

Meditating as a Christian

Collins

First published in Great Britain in 1991 by
Collins Religious Division,
part of HarperCollins Publishing
77-85 Fulham Palace Road, London W6 8JB
Copyright © 1991 Peter Toon
ISBN 0 00 599189 7

Printed and bound in Great Britain by
Collins Manufacturing, Glasgow

CONDITIONS OF SALE

Contents

Preface

I offer this book to all who are seriously interested in the subject and practice of meditation. In particular I offer it to those who want to know what is authentic Christian meditation. Though of necessity I have had to use some technical terms, I have tried to write in such a way that a person of average intelligence can easily follow my presentation.

Perhaps I ought to admit that the writing of this book has given me both joy and pain.

The joy has come as a result of surveying the way that both the biblical writers and Christian teachers have written about meditation as a waiting upon the Lord and a way into the knowing of the God and Father of our Lord Jesus Christ. I have been especially happy to see a deep similarity in the path of meditation used in the Orthodox, Catholic and Protestant Churches, in each case centred upon the Word made flesh, Jesus Christ our Lord. This joy is reflected in the title, *Meditating as a Christian*.

The pain has come through my having to make the decision to advise people to be most careful in the use of, and, in some cases, to set aside that path and those forms of meditation which are based on Hindu and Buddhist philosophy (see chapter one). Many sincere people – often unwittingly – have begun to use them as if they were neutral and could be adapted to the service of Jesus Christ; and it would appear to be the case that Eastern methods and techniques have made great inroads into Roman Catholic convents and monasteries (see the Roman Catholic international monthly, *30 Days*, September 1989, and the article "The Yoga Connection").

I see this book as covering a much broader canvas than my earlier books – *From Mind to Heart* (Baker Book House, 1987) and *Meditating Upon God's Word* (Darton, Longman and Todd, 1988). I offer it as a general introduction to Christian meditation in the context of the current religious and cultural situation in the West. Further I shall be delighted if what I write is of service to Christians of all denominational allegiances as well as to people of none.

Though, of course, I am personally responsible for what I have written, I would like to express my thanks to my wife, Vita, to Stratford Caldecott of Collins Publishers, and to John Saward of Ushaw College, Durham, for their general encouragement; and to two parish clergymen, Peter Dodson and Richard Ginn for their helpful comments on early drafts of the manuscript.

Prologue

The themes of being silent before, and waiting upon the Lord, run through the Bible as a rich vein. They are well expressed in the opening verses of Psalm 123:

I lift up my eyes to you,
  to you whose throne is in heaven.
As the eyes of slaves look to the hand of their master,
  as the eyes of a maid look to the hand of her mistress,
so our eyes look to the LORD our God,
  till he show us his mercy.

The Psalmist looks through and beyond the hills, the skies, and human activity to the transcendent God, whose home is in heaven, and whose Spirit is present in and through creation. By faith he sees the Creator and Preserver of the cosmos, the Redeemer, Father and Judge of Israel.

The way he looks and waits in silence is important. To appreciate this, he asks us to imagine the palace of an eastern prince. First, we are to see the slaves standing still and quiet, watching their Master with great care in case he should beckon with his hand. We are to try to imagine the attitude and feelings of the slaves. In the second place, we are to see the young slave-girl acting as the maid of the princess. We are to try to imagine how she is trained to watch her mistress with great care and attention, ready to respond to the slightest instruction from the move of her hand.

We are to wait upon God, to look to the Lord, in this manner and much aware that we are his creatures, his servants, and, alas sinners as well. So we look to our Creator, Preserver and Judge for mercy, for a right relationship with him that includes forgiveness and communion. We wait in silence, in faith and expectantly for signs from his hands – signs of grace, signs in nature and signs in providence. We set apart a fixed time daily and look for further opportunities throughout the day specifically to wait upon God and to watch for the movement of his hands of mercy.

God has made himself known by word and deed to and in the history of the people of Israel, in the person, ministry, death and resurrection of Jesus, and in the life of the Church. Our eyes are to look to the Lord as he is revealed here (as recorded in Holy Scripture) in grace and in mercy. Secondly, God's eternal power and divine nature are revealed in and through the natural order; as we survey this we are to see through the physical reality to the merciful hands of God and the dynamic word of God, by which it came into being and by which it is sustained and renewed. In the third place, we are to look at the events of our lives and see the gracious hands of God guiding and controlling what happens to us day by day.

This looking by faith can be called mental prayer or meditation or even contemplation. It is a fundamental part of Christian believing and living and without it prayer as dialogue or communion with God is partial or paralysed. It has been said that a daily Christian life without meditation is similar to a cut flower which, even if it is carefully placed in a vase filled with water, can only keep fresh for a short time. Thus meditation ought to be such a fixed part of our lives that we engage in it regularly, just as we have fixed times for breakfast, lunch and dinner. We need to say each day to our Lord: "This time is for You and for you alone. I want to wait upon you, be with you and meditate upon the signs of your mercy which you offer to me".

In explaining and commending the Christian practice of meditation this book is divided into four parts. In the first, "What it is", the Christian meaning of meditation is assembled and it is shown to be part of our Lord's will for our busy lives. In the second, "How it works", we look at possible ways in which the practice of fixed and occasional meditation can be undertaken. The third and longest part, "What is involved", examines what the act of meditation can mean for the physical body, mind, heart and will. Then the final part takes up the relationship of meditation to academic bible study and theology and contemplative prayer.

I hope and pray that those who "persevere" to the end will be able to say that they have been helped to see more clearly what waiting upon the Lord our God means today.

PART 1

What it is

1
Meditating . . .

Perhaps like me you find the modern usage of the word "meditation" rather confusing. People employ it today in contexts as different as bodily relaxation, mental exercise, and a spiritual discipline within a religious context. As a Christian pastor/teacher I have chosen to write on the theme of meditating as a Christian.

So I shall only deal with other forms and types of meditating to the extent that is necessary in order to make crystal clear what in fact it is to meditate Christianly. My main aim is to describe and commend the practice of meditating within a definite Christian (trinitarian) commitment. However, to achieve my aim, I believe I need to offer some basic information about other forms and types of meditating. This is because the nature of any particular thing or system is often clearest when contrasted with other related or similar things or systems.

RELAXATION

First of all, meditation can mean exercises which aim at relaxing the whole person and thereby making the participant a healthier and more stable person. Examples of this are simple, popular Yoga classes (in England often offered as evening classes to the general public) and the apparently still popular (with business people) Transcendental Meditation. At one level we may see this form of meditation as being a kind of keep-fit exercises for the mind/soul and thus parallel to keep-fit classes for the body.

There seems to be little doubt but that by the use of certain techniques – control of breathing, right bodily posture and the constant daily repetition of a single word or short phrase for a specific period of say fifteen minutes daily – the human mind can be stilled and the whole body relaxed. For the activist westerner this is often such a refreshing experience that it can have all kinds of beneficial side-effects. These range from the lowering of blood pressure to becoming a more attractive and successful business-person. So it is hardly surprising that, in order to attract westerners, adverts for courses in Transcendental Meditation describe it as "a simple technique for realizing your full mental potential and attaining a deep sense of rest".

It is possible with both Yoga and Transcendental Meditation to use their preliminary techniques and ignore their religious dimension – the doctrine/philosophy within which they were developed and with which they are still very much connected in mother India. However, the minority who go on past the initial, basically physical exercises, soon become aware that they are definitely in a religious context, with a special vocabulary and belief systems.

Further, there appear to be a growing number of medical doctors who use meditation as a therapy. Herbert Benson MD of the Harvard Medical School is one of the best-known through his book *The Relaxation Response* and other titles. He uses the word "meditation" of a non-religious exercise which is designed to help a person to overcome fatigue and stress, cope with anxieties, sleep well, be alert, and deal with what has been called "the fight-or-flight response". Adapted from the initial stages of Eastern religious meditation, the technique is simple and works! Here it is:

1. Choose a focus word or short phrase which may or may not come from your belief system (e.g. a Jew may choose "Shalom" and a Christian "Jesus" and an agnostic "hopefulness").
2. Sit quietly in a comfortable position.
3. Close your eyes.
4. Relax all your muscles, beginning at your feet and progressing up to your face. Keep them relaxed.
5. Breathe through your nose: become aware of your breathing; repeat the focus word silently to yourself as you inhale and exhale: breathe easily and naturally.
6. Continue for between ten and twenty minutes; and do the exercise at least once a day.

It is most important, Dr Benson tells us, to maintain a passive attitude by not chasing distracting thoughts or dwelling on them but simply continuing calmly to say the focus word.

RELIGIOUS DISCIPLINE

In the second place, the practice of meditation is found in all major religions of East and West. One has only to be slightly familiar with both Hinduism and Buddhism to be aware of the emphasis placed upon meditation as the way to enlightenment, pure consciousness, bliss, ultimate reality, the Self, and "God-realization". Deep within the human soul, it is held, there is a hidden treasure to be found; to reach it is not only to gain freedom through self-realization but also to encounter Brahman or "that beyond which there is nothing else or more". Visitors to the Indian sub-continent are often greatly impressed by both the bodily postures and the tremendous self-control manifested by those who engage in such meditation.

The Scriptures of the Jews (= the Christian Old Testament) also amply testify to the importance of meditation. When Joshua took over the leadership of the tribes of Israel after the death of Joshua, God commanded him to meditate. "Do not let this Book of the Law depart from your mouth; meditate on it day and night, so that you may be careful to do everything written in it" (Josh.1:8). This command became part of the requirement for genuine piety within Israel as is seen from the contents of Psalm 1, which is an introduction to the whole Psalter (the Jewish prayer/meditation/song book). "Blessed is the man . . . (whose) delight is in the law of the LORD, and on his law he meditates day and night" (v.2). Christianity inherited meditation as a spiritual discipline from Judaism and its practice within the Church in all areas and times has been fully documented. It has been particularly, but by no means exclusively, associated with the monastic movement. The purpose of all Jewish and Christian meditation is to come to know the God who has revealed himself to mankind. And this meditation at least begins from a sacred text. We shall have much more to say about this later in the book.

UNDERLYING DIFFERENCES

Thirdly, though the one word "meditation" is used, the actual spiritual discipline which is called meditation is not identical in all religions. There is, however, a distinct similarity in meditation in Hinduism and Buddhism on the one hand, and in Judaism and Christianity on the other. The simplest way to highlight the difference is to say that for the one meditation is an inner journey to find the centre of one's being, while for the other it is the concentration of the mind/heart upon an external Revelation. For the one revelation/insight/illumination occurs when the inmost self (which is also the ultimate Self, the one final Reality) is reached by the journey into the soul, while for the other it comes as a result of the encounter with God in and through his objective Revelation to which Holy Scripture witnesses.

In both Judaism and Christianity meditation is always paying attention to, and responding in mind, heart and will, to the God who has made and makes himself known. For the Jew it is pre-eminently his revelation in the Law; for the Christian it is pre-eminently his revelation in Jesus, the Word Incarnate. In this sense meditation is upon that which is external to oneself – even though the believer is to receive the word of God into heart/mind and cherish it. For Christians, the Word made flesh upon which meditation is centred (through the witness to him of the New Testament) is at the right hand of the Father in heaven; yet, and here is the key to Christian talk of the interior life, Jesus is present in the soul in and through the indwelling Holy Spirit. Meditation is, then, for Jews and Christians thinking about, reflecting upon, considering, taking to heart, reading slowly and carefully, prayerfully taking in, and humbly receiving into mind, heart and will that which God has revealed. For the Christian meditating Christianly is being guided and inspired by the indwelling Spirit of Christ in the consideration of God's revelation.

Of course in Hinduism and Buddhism there is both the reading and study of holy books – though this is normally only for the minority. However, meditation refers to the use of specific techniques to cause the mind/heart to look and journey inwards to find the key to existence deep within one's own self, for there is no "God" to be discovered elsewhere. The methods taught and used have been developed over the centuries in the context of certain religious beliefs and to achieve certain spiritual ends.

ULTIMATE BEING

In the fourth place, it is perhaps now clear that beneath the very different forms or types of meditation are two vastly different concepts of what is ultimate being. That which undergirds most forms of meditation taught by Indian gurus who are popular in the West is a system called monism. Trees, stones, hills, valleys, animals and people are only diverse manifestations of the same One Consciousness. It is "Pure" for it is beyond thought, reason, emotions, will and morals. Further it transcends personality and is therefore impersonal. This Pure Consciousness, Ultimate Reality, Brahman, or Shoonya can be called "God" but this is definitely not to be understood as a personal God.

The only way to see this Oneness is to go beyond, that is to transcend, reason; for intellect is the chief villain which divides the One from the many. Through meditation as an inner journey into the soul, setting aside all distractions, you see Pure Consciousness for you actually become Pure Consciousness. That is, you are the arena where the Pure Consciousness becomes aware of Itself: therefore this state of inspiration of enlightenment can be called both self-realization or God-realization, since the real self is none other than the true Self (= God). But perhaps all this is better said through a simple story, which illustrates what enlightenment is – a conscious realization of the nature of one's own being.

A fisherman asked his spiritual teacher how he could achieve enlightenment. The teacher gave him a sieve and said that reaching enlightenment was like filling the sieve with water. The mind was like the sieve and when it was full then enlightenment would be achieved. It seemed rather disheartening but the fisherman had great faith in his teacher and so he thought long and hard as to what he could possibly mean. But he could not work out its meaning and so returned to his teacher to ask him to explain. He said nothing but took the sieve down to the water and immersed it in the water so that it was permanently full.

For Jews and Christians God is both transcendent (above and beyond the universe) and immanent (present within and through the universe). He is both the Creator and Sustainer of the world; it is wholly dependent upon him and further he is its Judge. As the living God he is personal Being and relates to believers in a personal way. This is expressed in the addressing God as "Father" because one is his child and as "Lord" because one is his disciple. It is the very basis of prayer which is a dialogue between (unequal) persons, of whom the one is the Creator and the other the created; however, the created is made "in the image and likeness" of the Creator and thus made for communion and fellowship. Thus meditation is a prelude to prayer. It is seeking to hear and know what God is saying through his (already given) Revelation in order to be able truly to engage in prayer, which is communion between the Creator and the created.

The Christian doctrine of God as Holy Trinity is all

about a God who is personal for he is a Trinity of persons in communion with each other; because he is gracious this personal Godhead draws into fellowship with himself forgiven sinners. They come to the Father through the Son by the Holy Spirit and thus have fellowship with the Father and the Son through the presence of the indwelling Spirit in their hearts.

It is probably true to say that the doctrine of God which a person holds will determine (certainly in the long if not in the short term) both the type and the method of meditation a person adopts. Certainly, if one holds or is attracted to a monistic view of reality then a form of meditation is required to take one away from the normal (unreal) world of sense perception to the inner (real) world of universal unity. However, if one believes in a God who is truly transcendent and who only lives in the human soul by grace and upon his own conditions, then a form of meditation and prayer is required which aims at entering into communion with this deity.

SYNCRETISM

Fifthly, there is a definite adoption of Eastern Hindu and Buddhist methods (which are often also mistakenly claimed to be much the same as Eastern – Greek Orthodox – methods) of meditation and prayer by Christian teachers, in order, it is held, to make the practice of Christian meditation more effective. The general presupposition here seems to be that there is a cluster or collection of techniques/methods/ways of meditation which have developed over long centuries in East and West. These are viewed as basically tools or instruments for achieving certain goals. In and of themselves they are neutral and can be put to any purpose, just as a ruler can be used both to draw a straight line and to measure a pencil. Since, therefore, it is held that the methods are sound, what is emphasized is the right motive in using a particular method or technique.

In the last twenty years there has been a continuing stream of books with titles like *Christian Yoga*, *Exploration into Contemplative Prayer*, and *Zen and Christian Mysticism* (often written by members of religious orders) which have commended Eastern methods for Christians. Perhaps the simplest form of an adapted "Christian Meditation" is that developed by the late John Main and associated with the Benedictine Priory he founded in Montreal and the meditation Centre in London. Everything begins from this starting-point:

> "Sit down. Sit still and upright. Close your eyes lightly. Sit relaxed but alert. Silently, interiorly begin to say a single word. We recommend the prayer-phrase, 'Maranatha'. Recite it as four syllables of equal length. Listen to it as you say it, gently but continuously. Do not think or imagine anything – spiritual or otherwise. If thoughts and images come, these are distractions at the time of meditation, so keep returning to simply saying the word. Meditate each morning and evening between twenty and thirty minutes."

This use of an eastern technique with a Christian focus-word or mantra, "Maranatha", is usually set in the general context of Roman Catholic worship. Main freely admitted that he picked up the technique from a Malaysian (Indian) guru; but he also held (in my view mistakenly) that it was a method sanctioned by the early, Egyptian desert fathers (as they are reported by John Cassian in his influential book,

Conferences). In fact, it seems to me that it can be (and maybe is) for some a way to achieve "the relaxation response" and is thus a helpful activity which in the right context can and does prepare a person to engage in Christian prayer to a God who is both transcendent and immanent.

However, I do believe that eastern techniques are often taken over either too uncritically or for the wrong reasons by some who use them. For example, some people from a Christian tradition use them because they have a doctrine of God which has little or nothing in it of divine transcendence and which locates God virtually totally in, with and through the created order – and is thus immanentist, panentheist or pantheist. Therefore their doctrine of God has definite similiarities with the Hindu philosophy of monism. Thus they meditate in order to make an inner journey to find God as universal Spirit in their souls. For this is the only sure place to find him, if he has not given a sure, external Revelation via Word and Sacrament!

I find it very difficult to justify Christian use of eastern methods of meditation, for two basic reasons. First of all, my doctrine of God includes both his transcendence and his immanence: the two belong together and the former is denied (or made irrelevent) by the practice of eastern meditation. Secondly, I do not believe that techniques/styles/methods of meditation (passed a certain point) are neutral like tools which can be put to a variety of purposes. I believe that the Christian tradition (in East and West) has developed forms of meditation appropriate to its doctrine of God, and in particular the doctrines of the Trinity and the Incarnation, and that Christians ought to use these, and only these methods. This is not to say there is nothing to learn from eastern experience of relaxing and being quiet; but, it is to say that in terms of the basic knowledge of God eastern meditation is intended to find a Reality, which to Christians is something (to say the least) grossly inferior to Yahweh (God, the Holy Trinity). Put in geographical terms, I cannot see how the river Jordan benefits from having the water of the Ganges flow into it. It serves only to make the Jordan cloudy!

[Note. Since writing this chapter the Congregation for the Doctrine of the Faith has released an important document on this topic, which I commend. It is *A letter . . . on some aspects of Christian Meditation* (Vatican, 1989).]

2
As a Christian . . .

We have suggested that the methods of meditation in Buddhism and Hinduism are determined by their teaching concerning ultimate reality. In fact they are designed to bring the devotee into the very essence of that for/at which the religion aims by its spiritual discipline. While aspects of the methods may be used for other purposes – e.g. bodily relaxation in a secular context – there is no doubt that the experience of centuries of practice makes them most efficient in bringing the devotee to that deep, inward experience or reality for which he seeks.

In this chapter I want to emphasize that the use of meditation in Christianity has been and ought to be primarily determined by the central teaching of Christianity. In other words the essential character of the Faith has provided and continues to provide both the purpose and thrust of methods of meditation. Further, I want to go on to say that Christians today ought not to use any method of meditation which is not wholly harmonious with the central thrust and teaching of Christianity.

GOD AS FLESH AND BLOOD

First of all, Christianity is based and centred upon Jesus Christ, who is confessed as the eternal Son of God who became Man as Jesus of Nazareth. He was born of the virgin Mary, took our flesh, assumed the role of Jewish

Messiah, suffered, was crucified and buried, rose bodily from the grave and in his new resurrection body ascended into heaven. In, with and through Jesus, the Messiah, God the Father povided/provides both revelation and salvation, in the power of the Holy Spirit. The opening verses of the Letter to the Hebrews put it in these words:

> "In the past, God spoke to our forefathers through the prophets (from Moses to Malachi and John the Baptist) at many times and in various ways, but in these last days he has spoken to us by his Son, whom he appointed heir of all things, and through whom he made the universe. The Son is the radiance of God's glory, and the exact representation of his being, sustaining all things by his powerful word. After he had provided purification for sins, he sat down at the right hand of the Majesty in heaven. So he became as much superior to the angels as the name he inherited is superior to theirs".

Jesus brought to fulfilment what God had revealed to the prophets of the old covenant – especially to Moses in the Torah – and then expanded that divine revelation through what he was, said and did. Therefore, because of who he is and what he has said and done, he is the Mediator of the new covenant: no one is able to enter into communion with the Father except in, through and by him. Meditation is in his name and for his sake.

THE GODHEAD AS HOLY TRINITY

In the second place, Christianity teaches with Judaism that God is One; there is only one Godhead/deity. However, it continues by affirming that God has made himself known to us as a Trinity of Persons (Modes of Being) whose names are Father, Son and Holy Spirit. This trinitarian confession is made by Christians because it was an irremoveable and irrepressible aspect of the Revelation provided by the living God in and through the ministry, deeds and person of Jesus. He spoke of "my Father" as being in heaven, of himself as the unique "Son" and of the "Spirit" whom the Father and Son would send into the world after his own exaltation to the right hand of the Father. Further, one of his last commands to his disciples was to go into the whole world, preach the Gospel, make disciples of all nations and baptize them "in the name of the Father, of the Son and of the Holy Spirit".

By having such a doctrine of God, Christianity emphasizes that God is personal. As the One God, he enjoys personal relations within his own Godhead in terms of the love of the Father for the Son in the Holy Spirit, who is the Bond of Love. Further, as the One God, the Father reaches out through the Son (who shares our human nature) and by the Holy Spirit to draw believing sinners into fellowship with himself and to become his adopted children, members of the "Household of Faith" and of the "Body of Christ". Thus, for Christians the ultimate Reality is not impersonal (as in eastern monism) but eternally and graciously personal. In meditation the aim is to be in dialogue and fellowship with the Father through and in the Son by the Holy Spirit.

THE SACRED SCRIPTURES

Thirdly, Christianity has always insisted that this One God who has graciously revealed himself has also caused a record and witness of that Revelation to be made. This record/witness to divine revelation is what we call the Holy

Scriptures. In the Old Testament is the record of God's revelation in the old covenant and specifically to Moses in what is called Torah or Law. Then in the New Testament is the record of God's self-revelation in Jesus, the Christ, who is the Incarnate Son. Thus knowledge of God, his character, will, purpose and ways is found in the Scriptures. Though there is a knowledge of God to be gained by the study of nature (including human beings), Christians have always insisted that the guaranteed source of knowledge is the Bible of the Old and New Testaments.

The Bible is God's book, kept and preserved by the Church of God. Guided by the Holy Spirit, the Church through specific members translates, interprets and makes available the Scriptures. The Scriptures are read in the services of worship as the Word of God: sermons are preached from the Word of God with the intention of being a message from heaven to the faithful worshippers, and the Gospel narrated in the four Gospels is declared by the Church to the world in its evangelistic mission. The attitude of the Church to the Bible is well set forth in the Collect for the Second Sunday in Advent of the *Book of Common Prayer* (1662).

"Blessed Lord, who hast caused all holy Scriptures to be written for our learning; Grant that we may in such wise hear them, read, mark and inwardly digest them, that by patience, and comfort of thy holy Word, we may embrace and ever hold fast the blessed hope of everlasting life, which Thou hast given us in our Saviour Jesus Christ. Amen."

In meditation there is a reading, a marking (=noting content) and inwardly digesting of their truth in order to stay in true knowledge of God.

29

COMMUNION WITH GOD

In the fourth place, Christianity insists that God offers to each repenting and believing sinner not only forgiveness but also a right and harmonious relationship with himself. Further, to create and cement this relationship, God himself in the person of the Holy Spirit comes to dwell in the soul of each believer. This divine presence makes it appropriate to refer to a Christian as "a temple of the Holy Spirit". His presence is an effective sign of salvation, a helper in prayer, a giver of true hope, a sanctifier of life, an enlightener and illuminator. However, since the Holy Spirit is the very Person of the Holy Trinity who inspired the writers of Holy Scripture, he also works invisibly within the human soul always in accordance with the teaching and principles set forth in the same Scriptures. There is perfect harmony between Word and Spirit.

The presence of the Holy Spirit within the forgiven soul certainly means that God may be said to be "in the depths of our being". However, he is present (as Jesus made very clear in John 14-16) as the Spirit of the Son sent by the Father and the Son. He is never owned, as it were, by the soul in whom he dwells. For he is God, the Third Person of the Holy Trinity, and his presence in the human soul is always and only that of divine Gift. The practical point that arises from this is that to look into the soul for God is certainly to find him but to recognize immediately that he is not owned or controlled by the believer. For he who is Guest is also King of kings and it is in him that we live and move and have our being; he comes to dwell because he has made man in his own image and after his likeness. Communion with him in the depths of the soul is not a communion of equals but a fellowship of Creator and created, Father and child, Bridegroom and bride. Thus Christian spirituality is never only inward-looking for it must always also be a looking in faith unto Jesus, the author and perfector of our faith. Further, the inward journey is not an isolated movement; it occurs in parallel with the faith that looks outwards and upwards to heaven and to the exalted Lord Jesus Christ, the Advocate and High Priest of the believing people of God.

A FELLOWSHIP OF SINNERS BEING SAVED

The fifth point is that Christianity is all about a community (church) of people who have the vocation of loving, worshipping and serving God, the Father, through, with and in the Lord Jesus (by the Holy Spirit). Each of these prepositions is important. We, as sinners, can only approach God *through* Jesus for he is the "Way, Truth and Life" and no one comes to the Father except by him. He is the one Mediator between God and mankind, who by his expiatory death has made it possible for us to approach the Father as forgiven sinners. Further, we come to the Father *with* him. He has taken permanently to himself our human nature and though never ceasing to be truly God he is also truly man. It is with him as our leader, Lord, Pioneer, Guide and Friend that we travel the narrow way which leads into everlasting life. In fact he is with us on this journey for he is present to us by the Holy Spirit, his Paraclete, who is both within us and alongside us on this journey towards the heavenly city.

We are seen by the Father as being *in* the Lord Jesus, enclosed within his perfected and glorified human nature. In Jesus we died to sin at Calvary; in Jesus we were raised to new life and exalted to the heavenly life at the Father's right hand; and in Jesus we will be given new resurrection bodies at the end of this present age in order to live fruitfully in the new age to come.

To go to the Father through, with and in the Lord Jesus means that all we offer to the Father in terms of love, worship, prayer, obedience and faithfulness is taken up by the Lord Jesus and made a part of his constant offering of perfect love, worship and service to the Father in his office as our great high Priest. This is why we need the presence of the Spirit in our hearts. The Spirit unites the sacrifice of praise, prayer and service to that of the Incarnate Son and thereby what we offer is made acceptable to the Father. Thus it can truly be said of the people of God that they offer prayer and praise "through the mouth of Christ". And they do this, of course, especially in the celebration of the Lord's Supper, the sacrament of the body and blood of the Lord Jesus, who died but is now alive for evermore.

Thus meditation within Christian worship is wholly appropriate and can be based upon any aspect of God's character, purpose and will as that is made known through liturgy, Scripture, preaching, sacrament, hymnody, and prayers.

THE SACRAMENTS OF GRACE

Sixthly and finally, Christianity places a great emphasis upon sacraments – in particular Baptism and the Lord's Supper. These were instituted by Jesus Christ as the sacraments of the new covenant. Baptism is administered once to those whom God is admitting into the new covenant and into the fellowship of the Church, which is the household of faith and body of Christ. The Lord's Supper is the eucharistic service of the Lord's people around the Lord's Table and on the Lord's Day in order for the Lord himself to deepen and enlarge their communion and fellowship with him. Right reception of each sacrament demands from the forgiven sinner who is now an adopted child of God a total commitment of faith, trust, love and obedience.

God himself is present invisibly in and at the sacrament as the Spirit of Christ forging a deeper union and relationship of each participant with himself. However, though the divine presence is invisible to the physical eye, the signs of the presence – the water of baptism and the bread and wine of the Supper – are visible. Also there is the reading aloud of the words of institution and command. Signs are seen; words are heard; however, the Christ to whom they point and of whom they testify is the Incarnate Son, who is at the right hand of the Father in heaven, but made present in and by the Holy Spirit.

The sacred signs/symbols together with the Gospel word accompanying them provide an exciting and solid source of meditation. As I receive the body and blood of Christ I can picture him dying on the cross, breaking bread with his disciples after his resurrection, and standing behind the holy table/altar speaking directly to me, as I ponder and appropriate his words of grace.

REFLECTION

The question now arises: If this is, in general terms, an accurate account of Christianity then what kind of meditation is appropriate to it? Let us begin by noticing what meditation means in the Old Testament for this was the Bible of Jesus, the apostles and the first Christians. Here as a reading of the Psalter will make abundantly clear meditation is obviously the thinking about, considering, reflecting, learning by heart, working out the practical implications of, and musing upon the revelation given by God to Israel – especially the revelation given to Moses and as written down known as Torah.

This makes good sense. For if God has revealed himself, and if that revelation has been recorded and is available to be read, heard, and received, then the way to knowledge of God is obviously via the text, whose message must be prayerfully digested. Further, since it is such a precious text, it is appropriate to read, memorize and recall it as often and carefully as is possible. As far as I can tell there is nothing remotely like the eastern method of meditation recommended or illustrated in the Old Testament: and the reason is because of the Hebrew doctrine of Yahweh is that of a personal God who reveals himself to his unworthy people in words and deeds, who binds himself to them through a gracious covenant, and who blesses them even when they are undeserving.

Meditation within the new covenant is identical to that within the old in terms of the method: what is different, or extra, is that the mind/heart/will is being addressed through the words of the sacred text by a fuller, richer and greater revelation from God than was available to the faithful Israelite. Thus to gain a right knowledge of God and by divine grace to be in a right relationship with God meditation as the dwelling upon, the taking into mind and heart and receiving into the soul of the Word of God is, if anything, more important. For through the action of the Holy Spirit the receiving of the inspired words is in fact the receiving of Christ, the Word made flesh, who (in St Paul's language) dwells in the heart by faith. Again I must say that as far as I can tell there is nothing remotely like the eastern method of meditation found anywhere in the New Testament; and the reason is because God is perceived as a Trinity of Persons and the Second Person is known as the Word made flesh. Thus God calls sinners into communion with himself by the all-gracious and all powerful words of his Gospel, which is addressed to human beings for them to receive.

The knowing of God which is eternal life and salvation is a knowing which involves the whole person. It is certainly knowing the Truth which/who is Jesus himself; while such knowing is more than merely intellectual knowing it certainly includes an important intellectual or mental element. This is surely why both the Gospels and the Epistles are filled with doctrinal and ethical teaching. The way to God begins, practically speaking, through the hearing/reading and receiving of the Gospel which is the word of God. Meditation is a part of the process/means by which the Gospel/Word of God continually enters the soul as illuminating, liberating and saving word. The Word of God is for the whole person but not by excluding the intellect or mind. Rather it is the mind-in-the-heart thrusting the will to lead the whole person, body and soul, to act Christianly.

Meditation is therefore the prelude to both prayer and action for it is a divinely-appointed way of receiving the living word of the Lord into the heart/mind/will. It does not exist alone and it functions in various forms depending on the maturity and personality as well as the context of the person who meditates. Often in Christian teaching,

Mary, the Mother of our Lord and his first disciple, is presented as a model of meditation. She not only freely submitted to the word of God through the angel (Luke 1:38) but she treasured the word of God in her heart, allowing it to be the mainspring of her life (Luke 2:51).

3
Spirituality . . .

"Spirituality" is a word with many meanings in contemporary English. In fact what it means in any context is determined by the understanding or definition of "spirit". Is it the human spirit in one or another of its aspects and identities? Is it an evil or demonic spirit? Is it a universal, immanent spirit? Or is it the Holy Spirit, Third Person of the one Godhead of Father, Son and Holy Spirit?

EASTERN SPIRITUALITY

The methods/techniques of meditation (understood as an inward journey) practised over the centuries in Hinduism are, as we have noted, intimately connected with a view of ultimate reality/God. This view leads the devotee to expect to find ultimate Spirit deep within himself and to believe that an ascetic life is absolutely necessary to turn one's focus from the worldly and the fleshly to the inner true self, which is also ultimate Self/Spirit. We may note in passing that having the experience of the inner journey is one thing; describing it is another; and evaluating it is yet another! Within different strands of Hinduism and Buddhism there is a variety of descriptions and evaluations.

But how are we who live within the Christian tradition to evaluate such spiritualities? One common evaluation offered today by theologians in the Christian tradition is based on the doctrine that Jesus Christ is an inclusive Saviour. That is, God the Father gives his salvation to all

37

sincerely religious people, whatever their views and whether or not they believe that he is the Incarnate Son of God. This means, in effect, that all who sincerely practise eastern forms of meditation as an inward journey to their inmost Self will be saved by the universal grace of God.

However, if a Christian takes seriously the doctrine of God as Holy Trinity and of the Second Person of the Trinity, Jesus Christ, as the "Way, Truth and Life" and "only Mediator between God and man" then the evaluation must be different. Whatever attractiveness the spirituality may have it will be seen at best as a human attempt to reach God and at worst an example of error and delusion caused by Satan. Thus, in these cases, the "spirit" of the "spirituality" is either merely and only human spirit or human spirit deluded by evil spirit. Sincerity is not the key here: truth is the key!

The meditation being commended in this book is a spiritual discipline within a Christian Spirituality. The "S" is important, pointing both to the Godhead as eternal Spirit and to the Third Person of the Godhead, the Holy Spirit.

CHRISTIAN SPIRITUALITY

Christian Spirituality is travelling in the way of the Holy Spirit, who is the Spirit of Christ for and unto those who are united to the Lord Jesus Christ by living faith. It can be described as "reaching for the Ideal" and "aiming for the Goal". Here the Ideal and the Goal are the exalted Lord Jesus Christ, who (in his recorded teaching in the New Testament) called his disciples to follow him and in imitating him to be holy in purity, perfect in love and living in righteousness. Life filled with this aim is life offered to

God in worship, faith, faithfulness, love, obedience and service.

Spirituality is a personal involvement with and response to the God who reveals himself, and in so doing offers everlasting salvation to all who come to him in repentance and faith. Yet it is not merely a human involvement solely by human power and resources. It is rather the response of a believer who is ready and open to the enlightening, guiding and strengthening of the Holy Spirit. So "Spirituality", in an orthodox Christian context, may be said to be "the sphere of human nature in which the Holy Spirit is active as the Paraclete or Spirit of Jesus Christ, the Lord and Saviour, as the Sanctifier".

It is a personal but not an individualistic involvement with and response to the grace of God. An individual who accepts God's salvation freely offered in Jesus Christ becomes in faith/baptism/conversion a child of God and thus a member of the household/family of God. Another way of putting this is to say that a Christian is made a member of the "Body of Christ". This means that Christian Spirituality is a personal involvement and response within a community involvement and response. The community is of course the Church of God whose primary purpose on earth is to offer to God spiritual sacrifices – of worship, prayer, costly service, mission and evangelism.

Within this framework it is possible to envisage and to point to a cluster of Christian Spiritualities in which there is a basic unity without any uniformity. Within the Roman Catholic Church each of the religious orders has developed over the centuries its own particular form of spirituality, so that the Carmelite is not the same as the Benedictine, or the Jesuit the same as the Cistercian. Then there are different forms of Spirituality in the different Christian denominations (a charismatic and evangelical Spirituality in a Baptist setting is likely to be different in emphasis from a traditional Anglo-Catholic Spirituality in an Anglican context). Even within one denomination there often exist varied examples of Spirituality. This is particularly so in the Church of England well known for its comprehensiveness. Yet common to all is the recognition of the presence of and work of the Holy Spirit as the Spirit of Christ and the call of Jesus Christ to perfection of love and holiness/righteousness of life together as the children of God.

The differences in the varied forms of Spirituality appear not only in forms of public worship but also in the way spiritual disciplines are understood and undertaken. For example, for traditional Catholics and Anglicans fasting in Lent is an important discipline. In contrast, many evangelicals and charismatics do not consider it as a duty. Then, for evangelicals and charismatics the midweek meeting for a session of prayer and Bible study is a vital duty whereas to other Christians it may only be an option.

Even where there is agreement on the discipline there is not necessarily agreement on how it is to be undertaken. Take the duty of daily devotions, for example. One Christian may read the Bible with the help of published Notes and then offer prayer. Another may recite the written prayers within a Prayer Book and yet another may go daily to a parish church where there is a daily service. Yet here, I would say, there is a basic unity without uniformity, a unity in diversity. For we have to take into account not only that God has given to each of us an unique personality but also that he has placed us to live in differing cultures and traditions. The vocation to all everywhere in all traditions is "Be holy as I am holy" (see further my *What is Spirituality*, DLT., 1989).

Generally speaking we may say that much Roman Catholic spirituality is presented through the threefold way to God – (i) that of purgation/cleansing/purification; (ii) that of illumination/enlightenment/knowledge and (iii) that of union/contemplation/ecstasy. This way is initiated and made possible by the Holy Spirit who looks for human co-operation at all times. Thus, for example, much traditional material on meditation is structured to lead the beginner through exercises which help to get started and then to deepen the experience of being made aware of sin and purged of it. However, the three ways are not to be thought of as three steps of a ladder for in this life there will always be need of cleansing and further knowledge of God. However, it is true to say that the way of union or contemplation which includes spiritual communion with God and delight in his presence must be preceded by a process of cleansing and spiritual enlightenment. (See below, chapter 18.)

In contrast the primary way in which Protestant spirituality is presented is that of the dual process of mortification and sanctification. There is to be a constant putting to death of the thoughts and activities which spring from the old nature (the self in its own strength and inclinations); and there is to be a constant inflowing of the Spirit to illuminate, guide, strengthen the believer to love and to obey the will of God and thus be sanctified, made holy and conformed to the model of Jesus Christ.

MEDITATION AND SPIRITUALITY

Where, then, can we place meditation within Christian spirituality? We may say, *first of all*, that meditation is being attentive to God, a continuing involvement of the mind/heart with God's self-revelation. Thus it is to be related to all occasions/spheres/possibilities of encountering God, the Revealer. So, for example, meditation can be associated with hearing the Bible read or a sermon preached or a eucharistic liturgy celebrated; it can proceed from private reading of the Bible or other "holy" books (e.g. prayer books) or from being in/looking at what God has made (the creation) or of what God is doing in human lives (divine providence and self-examination). Further, it can be long or short and (if written down) in prose or poetry, and even expressed visually in art or by sounds in music.

In the *second* place, meditation is obviously not an end in itself. There is spiritual and even aesthetic delight for the believer in the considering of God's self-revelation to mankind. Yet she or he does not meditate in order to get mental pleasure; when it occurs it is a by-product thankfully received. Meditating is in order to know the will of God and gain the desire and determination to obey it. It is a means to an end and the end is the glorifying of God. The end or purpose ought not to be (in the first place) the creation or support of any human scheme – however good, but the knowing of God and being in communion and in tune with him.

Thirdly, meditation is to be placed somewhere in the pendulum of activity that lies between reverent study of the Bible (or creeds, catechism, liturgical books) and the dialogue with God we call prayer. In fact meditation may be called mental prayer. It is prayerfully reflecting upon, considering, thinking about God's character, word, will and ways in order to know him and serve him. But it is usually imposssible to state where meditation ends and prayer begins and where prayer ends and meditation starts again. The fact is that they run into each other, just as reverent Bible study also becomes prayerful meditation without any apparent intention to make it so.

In the *fourth* place, there are no absolute rules on how to meditate. There is plenty of advice in, say, Paul's Epistles on how to think about God's revelation in and through Christ Jesus; and a variety of methods for mental prayer/meditation were devised especially in the sixteenth and seventeenth centuries by European Christians. But most people need to start with one method or another in order to find out what method, simple or complex, suits them best. In chapters five to eight, I shall be discussing methods of meditation.

Fifthly, we need to say that there are no fixed rules as to the time for meditation. In Psalm 1 we are advised to meditate by day and night! It is possible to meditate while lying in bed, walking in the countryside, waiting for a bus, sitting in church, kneeling at the communion rail, flying in an aeroplane, feeding one's baby at one's breast, sitting in an office or peeling potatoes. The experience of the saints seems to tell us that we need to have a fixed time for specific meditation each day and then to meditate within services of worship and at other times as occasion arises and possibilities allow. Further there are no absolute rules as to length of meditation. What is long for one is short for another; so much depends upon individual personality and circumstance.

AN ABSOLUTE REQUIREMENT?

As yet we have not faced the important question: Is meditation as a spiritual discipline required by God, our Father, of all his children? Let us agree that all sincere

43

Christians accept that there is a duty laid upon them to hear and receive the Word of God, to receive the sacraments, to join in worship, to pray and to obey God's commandments (i.e. love God and neighbour). But not all would say that meditation is a duty. They would explain that there is no obvious divine command to meditate regularly and, further, not all people are capable of, or adapted to, meditation. All that is commanded, they would say, is that we hear and read the Word of God in order to obey it. We do not necessarily have to spend a long time musing upon God's self-revelation to us; rather we are to get on with the business of obeying our Lord in daily life.

There are Roman Catholics, Greek/Russian Orthodox, and Anglican Christians who think that meditation is a duty of monks and nuns but not of the ordinary laity. They see it as bound up with the daily monastic round of services, prayers and quiet. Then, there are conservative Protestants, who have a high doctrine of the Bible as the Word of God, but who think that meditation upon it is a somewhat dangerous exercise. This is because they suspect that it is seeking for meaning in the Bible that is not apparent in the actual literal meaning the text. For them, the meaning arrived at through basic historical and literary exegesis is the real meaning, and the meaning which God intends us to receive. Finally, we may mention those Christians who are so busy in what they believe to be God's work that they do not have time for meditation, which they see as a distraction from their duty to be up and active for Christ and his kingdom.

My own position is that it is a duty for all Christians: my reasons are supplied in the next chapter.

4
The Lord's Will . . .

In this chapter I want to attempt to show that meditation is a duty for all Christians. The only exceptions I can think of are small children, the mentally ill, the insane, and people suffering certain illnesses. Having made such a claim – rarely heard, I admit, these days – I need to say that I am referring to basic meditation (see what I say below about formative reading in chapter five and about the *lectio divina* in chapter eight) and not to any advanced method of prayerful musing upon God's revelation to us. Let me, however, go on to point out that what I say is not novel either in Roman Catholic or Protestant teaching.

HISTORICAL COMMENT

During the second half of the sixteenth and throughout the sevententh century both Roman Catholic and Protestant pastors placed before Christian people the duty each day of meditating upon God's revelation. The duty/practice was often called "the divine art of meditation". In this period Roman Catholics, as part of what is known as the Counter-Reformation, produced many books for the laity on the duty of meditation and prayer as a necessary and spiritually satisfying means of grace. One of the best known of these books is that by Francis de Sales, which I have had the pleasant task of editing for Protestant readers – *Introduction to the Devout Life* (Hodder, 1988; first edition, 1608).

Then we may note that the two great leaders of the Protestant Reformation at the beginning of the sixteenth century both saw daily meditation upon God's truth to be a divine duty. Martin Luther, who is now more appreciated in the Roman Catholic Church than ever before, wrote a marvellous little book on meditation and prayer entitled, *A Simple Way to Pray: for Master Peter, the Barber* (1535). Meditation on the Ten Commandments and the Lord's Prayer leads on to prayer so that the believer begins by being attentive to God's truth and then becomes through that Word intentive – wanting to wait upon the Lord and do his bidding. John Calvin, who regrettably is often judged by how people think of later "Calvinists", emphasized both meditation and prayer in the knowing of God in his classic presentation of Protestant teaching, *The Institutes of the Christian Religion* (1560). He insisted that God's call to be renewed in the image of Christ and thus be heavenly-minded can only be achieved by those who (along with other Gospel duties) learn to meditate upon what the sacred Scriptures teach concerning the Lord Jesus Christ, who is exalted at the right hand of the Father in heaven.

In fact within both Anglican and Puritan teaching in Britain (and New England) in the seventeenth century, meditation was taught as a duty for all Christians. It was presented in an abundance of books (regrettably now virtually forgotten) as that means of grace which, as it were, is the divine lubricator of the other means of grace – e.g. praying, hearing the preaching of the Word, receiving the Lord's Supper and personal Bible reading. This tradition of meditation as a daily duty continued in Protestantism (Anglican, Nonconformist, Lutheran and Reformed) into the nineteenth century. It was highly valued, for example, by the leaders of the Evangelical Revival in the eighteenth and early nineteenth centuries. However, the perceiving and teaching of it as a duty has weakened and virtually, but not wholly, disappeared in modern times. In some cases it has been replaced by the use of Daily Bible Notes. However, on the Roman Catholic and Orthodox side the practice of meditating within and alongside the daily offices has continued (even if in some cases changed in style by the influence of the "East") in religious houses, monasteries, seminaries and convents.

Though I heartily welcome the publication in various series today of spiritual classics from the past (see for example my *Spiritual Companions: An Introduction to One Hundred Spiritual Classics* (Marshall-Pickering, 1990)), I find it difficult to affirm that there is in either Roman Catholicism or Protestantism the beginnings of a revival of classic Christian meditation in the latter part of the twentieth century. Of course it is difficult to assess what is happening inside and outside the Churches; but there seems to be very little emphasis placed on biblical meditation within the theological training of the clergy/pastors today. It is, I think, true to say, that Martha (who was up and busy for Jesus before she really knew what he wanted) is more in favour than Mary (who waited to sit at his feet to find out what he wanted) in our churches today. We only want to hear/learn enough in order to get up and get going!

THREE REASONS

Having claimed that meditation upon God's revelation is a duty for all Christians I must now offer my reasons for such a claim. The reasons I offer come under several headings and I want to say that their cumulative effect is to cause the Christian to accept that meditation is a duty. My own view if that each of the reasons I offer is sufficient in and of itself to place the duty of meditation on our spiritual agenda; however, I recognize that different people are swayed by different reasons/factors and so I offer a cluster! However, before offering them I must again explain that I am speaking of basic meditation as a duty, not advanced meditation/contemplation.

1. Because Holy Scripture is inspired by the Holy Spirit

The writers of the New Testament obviously believed that the books of the Old Testament had a special, in fact an unique, quality. Paul speaks of the Jewish people as being entrusted with "the very words (= oracles) of God" (Rom. 3:2). Then he explains to Timothy that "all Scripture is God-breathed and is useful for teaching, rebuking, correcting, and training in righteousness, so that the man of God may be thoroughly equipped for every good work" (2 Tim. 3:16–17). Further, Peter taught that "prophecy never had its origin in the will of man, but men spoke from God as they were carried along by the Holy Spirit" (2 Pet. 1:21).

As reported by the writers of the four Gospels Jesus treated the Hebrew Scriptures as being the record of God's revelation to Israel along with the response of Israel to the divine self-disclosure. For example, in his time of testing/temptation in the Judean wilderness, Jesus answered Satanic suggestions with the confident assertion that "It is written . . ." meaning "God, himself, has said . . ." (Matt. 4; Luke 4). Further, he saw within the Scriptures prophecies/predictions concerning the Messiah of Israel which he saw himself fulfilling. In fact we may claim that he worked out the general nature of his ministry as Messiah through his own prayerful study of and meditation upon the

48

Scriptures. After his resurrection, in his conversation with two disciples on the road to Emmaus, we are told that "beginning with Moses and all the Prophets, Jesus explained to them what was said in all the Scriptures concerning himself" (Luke 24:27). Later he told others that "everything must be fulfilled that is written about me in the Law of Moses, the Prophets and the Psalms" (Luke 24:44). And, significantly, we are told that having made this claim Jesus "opened their minds so they could understand the Scriptures" (v.45).

Of course the claims made for Scripture by Jesus and his apostles were for what we call the Old Testament. However, it was a simple development of this approach to make even higher claims for the New Testament since this collection of books witnessed to Jesus, the Christ, who fulfilled the Law and the Prophets.

If it be the case – and this is the Christian claim – that the Bible, as containing the two Testaments, is inspired by God in its writing (we need not here go into the actual mechanics of how this inspiration occurred) then the interpretation and spiritual/moral appropriation of the contents of Scripture must also be within God's concern. He who inspired the writers must be he who also inspires the interpreters/readers – in each case, of course, via weak, human vessels. So it is this unique quality of Scripture as literature inspired by the Holy Spirit, and as pointing to Christ, which requires that it be studied and read prayerfully, believingly and with the help of the same Holy Spirit. I want to claim that meditation is part (certainly not the whole) of this process, for meditation is, essentially, a prayerful, humble, faithful reading or recalling from memory of this or that part of the Scriptures as the Word of God, with a view to knowing God. It may also be, of course, the paying attention to a truth (from the Creeds) which is based on God's revelation recorded in Scripture.

2. Because God commands that we love him.

When asked what was the most important commandment, Jesus replied (quoting the Law of Moses): "Hear, O Israel, the Lord our God, the Lord is one. Love the Lord your God with all your heart and with all your soul and with all your mind and with all your strength", and he added, "Love your neighbour as yourself" (Mark 12:29–31). If we compare what Jesus said concerning the loving of God with what is written in Deuteronomy 6:4–5 we find that the Law speaks only of heart, soul and strength, to which Jesus has added "mind" to make the command of God clearer. It is God's will that the human being loves God as a total person, with every part and aspect of his personality/body. The three Hebrew words – heart, soul and strength – represent the sum of the powers which belong to the total, composite life of man. The "heart" was in Hebrew psychology the organ of intellect while the "soul" was that of the desires and affections. "Strength" referred to all those bodily powers which are seen operative via the body. Presumably to make it clear that "heart" did include to the use of the intellect or the process of rational thought Jesus made the addition of "mind" (Greek, *dianoia*).

In order to love God that which has been revealed of God must enter the whole human person so that she/he in response can devote the whole self/being to God. One important way wherein God's truth enters the believer is through meditation: in fact, in the attempt to love God with the "mind" in the meditative, prayerful study of what God has done for us and said to us, the basis is laid for the love of God with "heart, soul and strength".

Let us also note the command of Jesus to his disciples that they "be perfect as [their] heavenly Father is perfect" (Matt. 5:48; cf. 19:21). Perfection means being complete in spiritual and moral maturity – total commitment, entire consecration and wholehearted dedication to the kingdom of God and to God's Messiah. In such places as the Sermon on the Mount (Matt. 5–7) and the Sermon on the Plain (Luke 6), Jesus filled out what perfection means practically. It is clear that it is only possible to be perfect, and to move towards perfection, by an ever deepening personal knowledge of God's character and will. For we can only love, trust and obey God if we know what such loving, trusting and obeying means; and if we are prepared inwardly to be moulded so that this is the kind of life we actually live. Again, meditation is an important means used by God both to help us see what perfection means in the mind and teaching of Jesus and his apostles and to give us the inner desire, determination and humility to press on towards that true maturity and complete personhood.

According to the Gospel of John, Jesus deeply desired that his disciples "know the Father" for this was to have eternal life (17:3). To know God is not only knowing about his nature, character, deeds, words, will and purpose. While certainly gaining such knowing of "facts" and "information", it is particularly a knowing which is a personal relationship, a personal communion with another. (In the Hebrew language "to know a person" can mean the intimate knowing involved in sexual intercourse.) Thus we are told that the Father "knows" the Son and the Son "knows" the Father and their knowing of each other within the trinitarian life of God is eternal and unique (8:55; 10:15). If knowing God is both knowing about him and knowing him in personal relationship, then more than mere informative reading or study of the Scriptures is necessary. They are to be studied but also they are to be prayed over, to be meditated upon, so that the knowledge which begins as information becomes also, through the action of the Holy Spirit, knowledge which is fellowship, communion and everlasting life.

3. Because God intends to renew our minds

What we call spiritual regeneration/new birth/birth from above is the beginnings of the work of the Holy Spirit in renewing our whole inner selves, mind, heart, will. St Paul, in particular, appears to emphasize the need for the renewal of the mind.

We note that after urging Christians to offer their bodies to God as a sacrifice of spiritual worship he continues: "Do not conform any longer to the pattern of this world, but be transformed by the renewing of your mind. Then you will be able to test and approve what God's will is – his good, pleasing and perfect will" (Rom.12:2). He had taught the Ephesians of the imperative need "to be made new in the attitude of your minds; and to put on the new self, created to be like God in true righteousness and holiness" (4:23–24). Obviously this renewing is primarily by the presence of the Holy Spirit for, as he also said, "those who live in accordance with the Spirit have their minds set on what the Spirit desires" and "the mind controlled by the Spirit is life and peace" (Rom. 8:5 and 6).

This renewal, the apostle emphasizes, is absolutely necessary for without the divine illumination the human mind (however well educated, sophisticated and enlightened) is unable truly to appreciate the excellency of the Gospel of God. In fact Paul expressed it more strongly when he wrote: "The god of this age has blinded the minds of unbelievers so that they cannot see the light of the gospel of the glory of Christ, who is the image of God" (2 Cor. 4:4)

The darkness caused by Satan and sin can only be removed by the power of the enlightening Spirit of Christ. However, the Spirit normally acts as the sanctifying Spirit in response to readiness and receptivity on our part. It is by hearing, reading and particularly meditating upon the Word of God that the Spirit becomes active in the renewing of the mind/heart. That is the Spirit purifies and renews through the spiritual and moral content of the written Word of God which in his use becomes dynamic and living; and we gain that content as we prayerfully read and sincerely ponder the content of the sacred Scriptures.

Speaking as a mature Christian on behalf of his colleagues in the apostolic ministry and of himself, Paul declared: "We have the mind of Christ" (1 Cor. 2:16). He meant that as led and guided by the Spirit, they were united to the exalted Lord Jesus in and by the Spirit, and thus were preaching and teaching what their Lord in heaven wanted them to preach. The evidence of Paul's letters is that he spent much time not only meditating upon the Old Testament but also reflecting upon what he had learned from the original apostles and first Christians concerning Jesus, his ministry, death, resurrection, exaltation and second coming. In fact the Epistle to the Romans may be called a theological meditation.

*

There is no specific command which reads "You shall meditate each day upon the Word of God". However in order to fulfil the commands of God which are revealed to us as his will for us, we must meditate upon his Word/

Truth regularly. For meditation is well described, as we have noted, as that means of divine grace which either lubricates or makes effective the other means of grace. This means that meditation is an excellent way into discerning the will of God and desiring to do it, an effective preparation for true prayer, an under-used method of preparing for public worship, a preparation for right receiving of the Lord's Supper, the positive use of a "gap" in one's busy life (e.g. waiting for a train/plane/bus) and a way of digesting the content of a sermon. In other words it is a divinely appointed means of acquiring the mind of Christ.

The proof of the pudding is in the eating, it is said; and this is true for meditation. Only those who actually practise it regularly actually know that (under God and with his blessing) it is a kind of divine oil lubricating all the spiritual disciplines and making communion with God and the serving of him more meaningful and satisfying.

PART TWO

How it works

5
Formative Reading

Since the word "meditation" is associated by most people today with the "East" and eastern religions, we perhaps need another word or phrase to convey that which is described as "meditating upon the Law (Revelation) of the Lord" (cf. Josh.1:8; Ps.1:2) in Scripture. The best phrase I have come across is "formative reading", an expression used by Adrian van Kaam, founder of the School of Formative Spirituality at Duquesne University, Pittsburgh.

However, to appreciate the force and meaning of "formative reading" we need to contrast it with "informative reading".

INFORMATIVE READING

We live in an age and civilization which takes for granted the availability of the printed/typed/handwritten page. There are books, booklets, newspapers, magazines, leaflets, and letters in abundance. Even the advent of television has not diminished their supply.

Most of this vast array of printed material exists to be read quickly – at least as quickly as any individual is able to read. We glance at the newspaper and read only those items which catch our attention. Business people read reports, summaries, letters, hand-outs and the like each working day. Students look through a variety of academic books, learned articles and reference works in order to prepare for examinations. In most of this activity we are gathering information or data, comparing and categorizing it as we proceed.

In this informative approach it is the individual who is in charge. Such reading of the printed word is basically utilitarian in approach. It is to gain information which will be useful to us in one way or another in life. And, as we see from regular advertisements, courses are offered on "speed-reading" in order to make us more efficient at the task of gathering and managing information.

Informative reading is obviously necessary if we are to live meaningfully in the modern world. Without it we would be marooned, isolated and out of touch. Further, informative reading has a place in the reading of the Bible. Christians surely need to read through whole books of the Bible in order to gain basic information about – say – the life and ministry of Jesus, or the apostolic career of St. Paul.

There is no single bodily posture with which informative reading is associated. It can be in the office chair, in the armchair, seated or standing in the commuter train or underground metro system, or even seated on the lavatory. It is done whether or not people feel comfortable and often out of necessity to fulfil duties and keep up with the pace of business.

FORMATIVE READING

The purpose of formative reading is to be "formed" by the text: that is, to be formed by Jesus Christ through the Holy Spirit, who both inspired and interprets the sacred text. Such reading is a way of allowing the Bible to become for the Christian the written Word of God. In contrast to informative reading, which requires that I, myself, be in control as I gather what I want or need to know, formative reading requires that Christ, my Master and Teacher who is the Incarnate Word of God be in control. He can be so through the Holy Spirit who acts in his name both through the text and in the soul of the reader.

In the formative approach I have moved from the fast lane to the slow lane and I have begun to function differently. I place myself in God's presence with God's written Word to hear what he has to say to me and to respond as is appropriate for a forgiven child of God. I am there to read slowly and dwell gently upon what is written by God for me. The whole exercise is an activity of prayer.

I do not hold the Bible in my hand in order to analyse, dissect or gather information from it. Rather I hold it in order to let my Master penetrate the depths of my being with his Word and thus facilitate inner moral and spiritual transformation. I am there in utter dependence upon our God – who is the Father to whom I pray, the Son through whom I pray, and the Holy Spirit in whom I pray.

Experience of the saints teaches us that it is best to read formatively a text/passage which we have previously studied or already read in our normal, informative style (or which has been looked at in Christian education). In biblical meditation it is wise to use a familiar passage so that we are not distracted by the need to know where a specific place may be found or who a given person is or what a particular word means.

Posture is important. It is probably best either to find a comfortable kneeling position (which conveys the sense of being a disciple of Jesus Christ who kneels before his Majesty) or a comfortable sitting position in a firm, upright chair (which conveys a sense of attentiveness and readiness to be taught and to learn). Other positions are possible as long as they are conducive to the aim of the meditation.

BEGINNING BIBLICAL MEDITATION

To read Holy Scripture formatively I must make space and time on a regular basis – preferably daily. Unless I have at least ten (better, fifteen) minutes set aside for this holy calling it is hardly worthwhile beginning. This is because moving into the slow lane from the activism of ordinary living involves a time of adjustment. Where there is a will there is a way and space and time can be found – even if it is only in the lunch hour in a city church. The fact is that biblical meditation is part of a total commitment to Jesus Christ as Lord and Saviour and is a necessary part of that waiting upon God, becoming more like Jesus, and putting first the kingdom of heaven which is required. Discipleship can be – usually is – costly for it creates for us a new life-style.

To begin, having entered a quiet place, I must sit comfortably on a firm chair with my back and head straight and my legs apart, not crossed. Other positions are possible, for example cross-legged on the floor with back erect. Or I must kneel comfortably – perhaps with back straight and sitting on my heels. I have been taught that God is always with me but I confess that I am not always aware of his presence. Thus having achieved bodily comfort and stillness (perhaps by using some breathing exercises), I must become calm as I recall that God is present with me. This can be done by saying slowly and aloud appropriate texts of Scripture – e.g. "Be still and know that I am God" – or by imagining Jesus entering that place and addressing a word of welcome (e.g. "I am with you always . . .").

Becoming aware of the presence of the Spirit of the Lord Jesus Christ with me I am then ready to offer a prayer that the inner content of the written Word will become the living Word for me and to me by the work of the invisible Spirit. This initial prayer is actually the beginning of a period of prayer for this type of meditation is intended to be truly a time of waiting upon God as his child and as the disciple of Jesus.

Turning to the chosen short passage (which I have previously read and perhaps studied) I think of it as if it were a short section, intended particularly for me, of a larger Letter sent from heaven to earth. The Letter is in fact a love letter, sent by the Beloved. Thus I am not to approach it objectively and scientifically but carefully and tenderly. I am to savour its every word and appreciate its inner and hidden meaning, which love can see, feel and know. I am now ready to begin to read formatively and meditate biblically in order to meet my Beloved. So I read aloud slowly the verse(s) chosen. One method is to notice the punctuation and to slow down and breathe more slowly for the commas and even more slowly for the full stops (periods, as Americans say), so I read aloud softly but clearly so that I may "taste" the flavour of the Word and may also hear the gracious sound of the Word. At the same time, my eyes see the content of the Word. And I read again – gently dwelling on each word, each phrase and each sentence.

My attitude is that of patiently abiding in God's presence and care and of listening and looking in humble expectancy. I may read my short piece of Scripture five or ten times or more – or less! Further, my reading will be interspersed by prayer – of praise or of petition or of confession. In advance I cannot plan what will be my involvement and response for I do not know what God is going to cause me to taste, feel, hear and see in his Word. On one day I may only read a few words for they become immediately a path into communion with God; but on another I may read several sentences before what I taste, see and hear becomes a channel of God's grace to me.

Of course, on some days this period spent in God's presence with his Word will seem to be more precious than others. However, it is a serious mistake to think that only when we have the most moving insights, illuminations, humblings and inspirations are we being spiritually renewed within. The saints tell us that times of seeming barrenness and darkness are also times of spiritual transformation. For the Word and Spirit are not dependent on our feelings even though God does graciously respond to our faithfulness in reading. The Word does enter into our hearts even when we do not feel that this is so for that entry is not dependent upon our feelings but on the gracious Spirit.

We perhaps need constantly to remind ourselves that the end and aim of formative reading is to seek Christ in the inspired and sacred text in order to discover the love of God, to savour that love and to be united in faith and love with the Bridegroom of our souls. My soul may be compared to the honey bee who gathers from the sweet, spiritual flowers of God's revelation the divine pollen in order to taste the heavenly sweetness of the salvation which is in Jesus. I read formatively so as to be moved in mind/heart, especially in my affective powers to desire, love and magnify the Lord, my God, in whom alone is my hope and salvation. This will lead to what we may call the application of the words of God to my situation. But, of course, I cannot know in advance what this will be for it will occur naturally.

There is a vocal lobby today insisting that we treat meditation as that spiritual discipline in which we engage to fortify us for involvement in such issues as those of conservation, peace and justice. Whatever be the merits of working to bring economics and ecology into harmony, for peace on earth and justice for all peoples, it is wholly wrong to set any agenda in advance for this time of formative reading. It is a time spent with the Lord our God in order to be drawn deeper into communion with him; therefore, we must allow him to be our Lord and not dictate what we expect from him.

We need to affirm that formative reading be done as a regular discipline. It is such a different way of reading to that in which we normally engage that we must persevere both to learn it and to keep proficient at it. It both demands and gradually creates in us gentleness and patience. Yet it is so demanding that most Christians will find that they are incapable of more than thirty minutes a day. Mature Christians will, of course, be able to meditate for longer periods both because they are experienced and because they have learned to begin to put into practice that which God has shown them in their meditation. This latter point is very important. God addresses us in and through Jesus Christ through the sacred text intending that we respond in worship and obedience.

Unless there is the readiness to worship, love and obey our Lord then there will be little joy and profit in formative reading. In fact, in this situation, slow reading will be merely slow reading and nothing else! It has been said that the devil is an expert at slow reading!

IN CONTEXT

In a normal Christian life, formative reading will be dependent upon not only a general, informative reading of Scripture but also involvement in a Church with its corporate worship, teaching of Christian faith and morals, and opportunities for fellowship and service. Without this context, personal, formative reading may get off target and be subject to personal whims and fancies. In fact controls, imposed by commitment within God's Church to the Creed, holiness and mission, are necessary. For, as part of God's general providential arrangement of our lives, they allow the Holy Spirit more effectively to minister to us as members of the household of faith which is the Church of God. God never intended that we go it alone; individual prayer/meditation is to be enriched by our participation in the fellowship of the Body of Christ.

Further, it is helpful for formative reading to be tied to whatever scheme of regular Bible reading we are using. Churches usually have lectionaries with readings from the Old and New Testaments for each day of the year. It makes good sense to read all or part of these and then let a part – but only a part – be the basis for the formative reading. There are no fixed rules. It is wise where possible to take advice from a mature Christian before choosing one particular method or approach. Methods are means to an end and the end – communion with God – must always be more important than the method. Because each of us is a unique personality any method of formative reading must be appropriate. Further, as we grow in grace we shall find that our approach/method will also develop and change. (Here we may find help in using specific methods of meditation developed in the sixteenth and seventeenth centuries [for which see chapter eight below] by both Catholics and Protestants.)

Whatever method we choose we must come to sacred Scripture ready to be placed at God's disposal and therefore keen to hear his Word. This keenness to hear may be compared with that of a mother for her baby. Before giving birth to her child she may have slept soundly through the loudest noise; but, after the birth, the child has only to rustle in the crib/cot and the mother will awake. Her keenness grows and matures in loving care and attention; and her care affects her senses so that she hears with new ears. In love of God and keenness to hear from him we, too, will develop new, inner ears to pick up his quiet voice, speaking to us words of grace both in our reading of the sacred text and in our times of prayer. We shall not always hear what we want to hear but we shall hear what is best for us and for the kingdom of God.

Another way of putting this is that if we begin formative reading with sincerity and commitment then our experience will be that of a deaf man who begins to hear and is full of joy at what he can hear, or a blind man whose sight is restored and is delighted beyond words with what he can see.

May the words of my mouth and the meditation of my heart be pleasing in your sight, O LORD, my Rock and my Redeemer (Psalm 19:14).

6
Quality and Quantity

Having looked at what may be called "fixed" meditation as a daily discipline, we now move on to look at a way of meditating/praying applicable throughout the whole day and night, recalling that we are bidden to pray without ceasing and to meditate by day and by night.

MANTRAS

The word "mantra" has entered everyday English recently. It refers to the chanting/saying over and over of a focus word or a phrase as a way into meditation. Not only is it used by groups who are deliberately adopting one or another form of an eastern religion (e.g. Buddhism or Hinduism) but it is also used by some Christians of their "prayer-word".

I believe that both for the sake of clarity and spirituality we need to distinguish between (a) the use of a mantra which is said continuously for a fixed period of time – say each morning and evening – in order to empty the mind and make "the inner journey" in search of the true self (see chapter one); and (b) the use of a short, meditatory prayer which is said often, perhaps at times continuously, in order to keep oneself always aware of God's presence above, around, with and in us. While (a) has its natural relation to a view of God which locates deity only in and through the natural order (e.g. monism, pantheism and panentheism), (b) has (or can have) its natural relation to a view of God which includes both his immanence and transcendence – trinitarian theism, for example, which is the Christian Faith.

In this chapter, I want to examine the latter use of the focus or prayer word/phrase. Since there is today a growing interest in the spirituality of the desert (Egyptian) fathers I shall look first at specific teaching on prayer/meditation passed on from them to the western Church by John Cassian; further, since there is also a fascination with Greek/Russian Orthodoxy in the West I shall look secondly at the "Jesus Prayer". I shall not notice here other similar doors into meditation – the traditional and much used rosary, especially by Roman Catholics, and the modern repetitive but prayerful singing of simple choruses or scriptural verses by communities like that of Taizé and within charismatic groups; but I do recognize that they can be and are ways into real prayer for thousands of people, old and young, today.

CONTINUOUS MEDITATORY PRAYER

In the fourth and fifth centuries some Christians left the respectability of the churches in the cities of the Roman Empire to seek to know and serve God in monastic communities in the deserts of Egypt and Syria. Their experience of their own selves, of each other, of the devil and especially of the Lord, their God, was heightened by their isolation. John Cassian (c.365–435) lived as a monk in Bethlehem and Egypt before moving to the West where he founded monasteries. In his book, *Conferences*, he sought to pass on to the West the spiritual wisdom he had learned from the desert fathers/monks. Our interest is

67

in the contents of the tenth conference, which has the general title, "On Prayer".

Cassian describes the conversation between Germanus, an inexperienced yet zealous monk, and his mature fellow monk, Isaac. Germanus desires to find a way of meditation/prayer by which it is possible to hold God in our minds continually in spiritual contemplation, and to do so without encountering continuing distraction.

Isaac provides a prayer formula which he claims has been handed down by some of the oldest fathers and which he gives only to selected souls. "To keep the thought of God in your mind you must cling totally to this formula for piety: 'Come to my help, O God; Lord, hurry to my rescue' (Ps. 69:2)." (This translation is not found in modern Bibles but it does capture the general meaning of the Hebrew original.) Then Isaac makes a series of important claims for the spiritual benefits coming to those who keep this prayer ever in their thoughts and pray it continually in all situations and moods in which they find themselves. Having described the benefits he proceeds to supply a variety of illustrations to show how the prayer-formula actually works. Here is one.

> I am troubled by the pangs of rage, of greed, of gloom. I am drawn to scatter that gentleness which I had embraced as my own. And so if I am not to be carried off by turbulent rage into bitterness I must groan mightily and call out, 'Come to my help, O God; Lord, hurry to my rescue'.

Of course, it is not to be said either within the mind/heart or aloud merely and only as a formula. Isaac explains that:

"The soul must grab fiercely on to this formula so that after saying it over and over again, after meditating upon it without pause, it has strength to reject and to refuse all the abundant riches of thought" – which do not flow from communion with God and the doing of his will. The continual saying of it provides opportunity to think of God/Christ our Saviour, of our absolute dependence upon his mercy and grace at all times, and of our need to be always open to his coming to us in order to help us. In this way the mind and heart are centred upon God and it becomes easier to live as a true disciple of Jesus Christ.

Isaac provides a powerful description of one of the effects of coming to maturity through continual meditation/prayer. "The zeal of his soul makes him like a spiritual deer who feeds on the high mountains of the Prophets and the Apostles, that is, on their most high and most exalted teachings. Nourished by this food, which he continually eats, he penetrates so deeply into the thinking of the psalms that he sings them not as though they had been composed by the prophet but as if he himself had written them, as if this were his own private prayer uttered amid the deepest compunction of heart."

Further, the "highest" blessing which the monk enjoys is "purity of prayer". Isaac explains: "This prayer centres on no contemplation of some image or other. It is masked by no attendant sounds or words. It is a fiery outbreak, an indescribable exaltation, an insatiable thrust of the soul. Free of what is sensed and seen, ineffable in its groans and sighs, the soul pours itself out to God" (we shall return to this "higher" form of prayer in chapter eighteen below).

Though this method of continuous meditatory prayer was intended for monks there is no reason why it cannot be adapted to the needs of Christians fulfilling a variety of vocations in the world. It seems to me that we, today, need not confine ourselves to this one verse from Psalm 69. One way forward would be to take a good, reliable, modern version of the Book of Psalms and to go through each psalm, looking for suitable prayer-formulae. Then, each person can choose one from the list and make it her/his meditatory prayer, using it when waking and going to sleep as well as often throughout the day. I do not think that such a prayer-formula should be used as a mantra, saying it continuously for a fixed period of time – eastern style (see chapter one). Rather, it is best to use it frequently and to pray it with the whole mind/heart/will so that it is really intended. Of course, it can be said several or many times on each occasion used; but, the intention is to mean it with one's whole personality, and not use it as a way of emptying the mind. We ought to say it in order to have God fill our minds/hearts with feelings and thoughts of his glory.

Verses which I think may serve as a prayer formula include the following: Psalm 4:1; 9:1; 19:14; 213:1; 25:1; 30:10; 38:21–22. But you may find it better to look for your own either in the Psalter or in the Epistles of the New Testament (e.g. "May the grace of the Lord Jesus Christ, and the love of God, and the fellowship of the Holy Spirit be with you" (2 Cor. 13:14)).

A final point to be made is this. This form of meditatory prayer is not meant to replace but to go alongside a fixed time for meditation/prayer. It is to be an outgrowth from as well as a feeder into the fixed, daily encounter with God through reflection upon his self-revelation, recorded in Scripture.

THE JESUS PRAYER

The prayer, "Lord Jesus Christ, Son of God, have mercy upon me, a sinner", has long been known and used by Orthodox Christians. It is now being discovered in the West as a prayer to be prayed continuously. The Jesus Prayer has links with two incidents recorded in the eighteenth chapter of the Gospel according to Luke. In the Parable of the Pharisee and Tax Collector the latter is described by Jesus as praying: "God have mercy on me, a sinner" while in the account of the healing of the blind beggar we learn that the beggar cried out to Jesus: "Jesus, Son of David, have mercy on me!"

Once more we need to emphasize that this prayer is not intended to be used as a rythmic incantation. The words are an actual prayer addressed to the Second Person of the Holy Trinity. Teachers from the Orthodox Church tell us that this Prayer functions at three levels of our consciousness. It is a prayer of the lips, said aloud but not chanted. Beginners are urged to say the Prayer slowly and carefully, taking care over each word; this can be done repetitively for ten or fifteen minutes once or twice a day, preferably in a quiet place. In the second place, the Prayer is to become a prayer of the mind, a meditation in which the content of each word is taken seriously by the mind in the context of knowledge (from Bible and Creed) of who Jesus is, what he has done/is doing for sinners, and one's own sinfulness. The transition from stage one to two happens quite naturally to those who persevere and who match their living with their praying. Finally, the Prayer is to become a prayer of the mind in the heart; here the Prayer, in some profound and inexplicable way, is lodged in the heart and the whole inner being is still; there is communion between Spirit and spirit, as the soul is focused upon God through Jesus, the Mediator. This final stage of prayer is not that of novices but is the gift of grace to those who have persevered lovingly in the art of divine meditation and prayer, at stages one and two.

It is true that monks on Mount Athos in northern Greece did develop particular ways of breathing to accompany the recital of this prayer. However, these techniques should only be used on the advice of a wise spiritual director who is totally familiar with them (see further *The Jesus Prayer*, by a Monk of the Eastern Church, St Vladimir's Seminary Press, 1987).

Apart from being used as a Prayer to be repeated slowly and gently, before, after or even during one's daily set devotions, this Prayer is, of course, ideally suited to be the Prayer for any emergency or the meditatory Prayer to use when there is time to fill in before the arrival of a bus, train, aeroplane or appointment. It is of such a character that a Christian can never grow out of its use, for the more we learn from Scripture and experience about the Lord Jesus Christ and our need of God's grace, so the more we can pray this prayer with fuller meaning and deeper intensity. Further, it is also a Prayer which a prayer-group can say together so that it becomes communally both a prayer on the lips and a prayer in the heart.

I find the expression, "the mind in the heart", used by the Orthodox to refer to the human source of true prayer, very helpful. For it points to prayer which, while not ceasing to be mental, is filled with emotion and commitment. Then it makes clear that the Jesus Prayer is not and was never intended to be a Christian form of a Hindu or Buddhist mantra. For this Prayer is offered from the very centre of human personality (in an outward direction, as it were) to the Lord Jesus Christ, who, while certainly dwelling in the heart of the believer through the Spirit and by faith, is truly exalted at the right hand of the Father in heaven.

*

The apostle Paul taught Christians to "pray without ceasing" (1 Thess. 5:17) and the continual daily and nightly use of either a prayer-formula from the Psalter or the Jesus Prayer are attempts to begin to obey this command. Of course there are other ways of meditating/praying continually – e.g. using different short prayers as occasion demands and memory supplies. Obviously Paul did not mean that we were actually and literally to keep praying for twenty-four hours a day. Certainly to live prayerfully all the time is possible; but, to pray continually is impossible. To illustrate: we say that a person has an incessant cough – but we hardly mean that there is actual non-stop coughing all day and night. Thus, we may say that prayer is to be like an incessant cough – it is always there ready to break out. This means that every corner of a person's life is to be touched with the spirit of prayer and the presence of God. Further, it means that there is increasing knowledge of God through constant, meditatory prayer.

In this sense – by the grace of Christ alone – there is both quality and quantity!

7
Short and Often

Here we look at further examples of what has been called "occasional meditation". The use of the scriptural verse, or the Jesus Prayer, or the rosary, as aids to mental prayer can be supplemented or totally replaced by other forms of meditation, which are not tied to a specific formula or repetition. In fact it is probably true to say that Protestant teachers of occasional meditation have not, in general, recommended the use of fixed formula – even biblical ones.

Short, occasional meditation is by its nature possible in a very wide variety of places, circumstances and times. One could fill a book listing these possibilities. Further, it can be undertaken in a variety of postures and with different methods. Bearing this in mind all that can be offered in a short chapter are some general examples and suggestions. It used often to be said that the proof of the pudding is in the eating; each Christian must develop her/his own way of meditating occasionally. I often think that retirement gives to Christian people a marvellous opportunity to develop this art of occasional meditation and thereby to fit themselves for the joy of heaven when they will contemplate the Godhead in his beauty in the face of Jesus Christ.

BUT WHY BOTHER TO DO THIS?

The answer has already been supplied in principle in chapter four; if it is the Lord's will that we ought to meditate then this must include both fixed and occasional meditation. If it is the Lord's will that we should pray unceasingly and live in a spirit of prayer, then this must require fixed and occasional meditation. If we are to keep ourselves aware of that supra-natural world where Christ is in glory then we must meditate occasionally to be aware that God is both Creator and Preserver of the physical and spiritual worlds and that in his Providence he guides the existence of each one.

In fact in order to obey the apostolic command not to be conformed to the passing wordly standards and aims (Rom. 12:1–2) of our generation and positively to be conformed to Christ, to be renewed in mind and to begin to think in his ways (Eph. 4 and 5), we cannot avoid the practice of occasional meditation. In fact the renewed mind of the Christian who is seeking first the kingdom of heaven will of its own momentum move into occasional meditation; this most acceptable tendency needs, however, to be supplemented by the creation of the habit of occasional meditation. That is, by a determination to use opportunities (in older English the expression was "to improve opportunities") and spaces in the day for reflection upon God's character, will, purposes and general revelation in nature, providence and everyday living.

For those who are able to express themselves in writing easily (prose and poetry) and whose normal lives provide the time, it is a good practice to write down their occasional meditations. In fact some people actually meditate better with a pen/pencil in their hands (I am not sure whether any do so sitting in front of their word processors!). The very act of writing down the first part of their meditation apparently has the effect of leading the mind on to further stages of reflection. We have in

Christian literature some fine examples both of meditative poetry (e.g. John Donne, George Herbert, Henry Vaughan, and hymnwriters such as Charles Wesley) and prose (e.g. the written meditations of Bishop Joseph Hall, Thomas Traherne and Benjamin Jenks – to mention only three of a vast number in the seventeenth and eighteenth centuries who either published or left behind written meditations).

EXAMPLES OF TOPICS AND SUBJECTS

Without attempting to be comprehensive I shall suggest some general areas where meditation has been found to be possible and effectual.

1. *"Look at the birds of the air . . . Consider the lilies . . ." (Matt. 6:25–34).* Reflection upon the contents of the natural order has been and remains a major source of occasional and even prolonged meditation. The Psalter provides examples of reflection upon God's revelation through the created order:

> The heavens declare the glory of God;
> the skies proclaim the work of his hands (Ps. 19:1).

With Christ living in the heart by faith then the glory within nature becomes even more glorious to the pilgrim believer:

> Heaven above is softer blue,
> Earth beneath is sweeter green;
> Something lives in every hue
> Christless eyes have never seen:
> Birds with gladder songs o'erflow,
> Flowers with deeper beauties shine,
> Since I know as now I know,
> I am his and he is mine.

This sight is still possible even where pollution has had its effects upon the earth and environment.

In his meditating upon creation Thomas Traherne wrote: "Your enjoyment of the world is never right, till every morning you awake in heaven, see yourself in your Father's palace, and look upon the skies, the earth, and the air as celestial joys: having such a reverend esteem of all, as if you were among the angels. The bride of a monarch, in her husband's chamber, hath no such causes of delight as you" (*Centuries*, I, 28).

In contrast, meditation can of course begin from the fact that God's world has been marred, polluted, poisoned, distorted and maltreated by human beings, usually in pursuit of greed! Such meditation could include reflection upon the creation as God intends it to be, the sinfulness of man which causes him to misuse this creation and the responsibility of man to put things right and act better in the future. However, it perhaps needs to be said that concern with the so-called "green" issues is not of itself meditation. Only when that concern is set within the theological context of God as Creator, Preserver, Redeemer and Judge does it take on the possibility of meditation.

Another fruitful area for meditation upon creation is to consider the human animal, man, both in the form of individual male and female and in community. A good place to start is Psalm 8:

> When I consider the heavens,
>   the work of your fingers,
> the moon and the stars,
>   which you have set in place,
> what is man that you are mindful of him,
>   the son of man that you care for him?

You have made him a little lower
than the heavenly beings
and crowned him with glory and honour.

The psalm proceeds to celebrate the place of man as ruler within creation, with responsibility for it as a trustee. I may ask myself to begin meditation: What is unique about man as an animal? How should human beings live in relation to each other and to the rest of the created order, and to God their Creator, Redeemer and Judge? Why is there not harmony within creation? Can there be harmony? What is the will of God for the whole?

2. *"Great are the works of the LORD; they are pondered by all who delight in them" (Psalm 111:2).* A large part of the pleasure and delight of the Christian life occurs through the observations of God's providence, particularly those which relate to personal and family life, and the life of the Church of God. For, as Paul put it, "we know that in all things God works for the good of those who love him, who have been called according to his purpose" (Rom. 8:28). To look back over a day, a week, a year, a lifetime and see the hand of God supervising one's affairs sending what he deemed right and allowing this or that to occur as he judged best is demanding but also rewarding.

It is especially rewarding if it is in the context of a life which is consecrated, handed over to, and committed to God (for what this means see that excellent book, *Self-Abandonement to Divine Providence* by J.-P. de Caussade). While pondering the right way to accept pain in life, Bishop Joseph Hall (who wrote the first classic text-book in English on meditation, *The Divine Art of Meditation*, 1606) came to this brief conclusion: "A man, under God's affliction, is like a bird in a net; the more it strives, the more it is entangled. God's decrees cannot be eluded with impatience. What I cannot avoid I will learn to bear" (*Meditations and Vows*, II, 1).

The once popular evangelical hymn puts the positive side of reflecting upon God's ordering of our lives rather neatly:

> Count your blessings, name them one by one,
> And it will surprise you what the Lord hath done.

It has often been said that without due observation of the way God's providence has been at work it is impossible for the believer rightly to thank and praise him. Further, our prayers of petition and intercession, for self and others, surely gain content and fervency through reflection upon God's care for us day by day.

In meditating upon God's activity in the ordering of our lives we need to keep in mind the advice of Proverbs 3:6. "In all your ways acknowledge God and he will direct your paths." That is we need to have an eye for God's care for us (1 Pet. 5:7; Matt. 6:32) as well as for the wisdom of God in the way he grants and withholds his mercies to us. The Psalter contains much advice through example on how to reflect on providence (see further chapter sixteen); those who use it regularly will gain much help in the way to meditate upon divine providence.

One of the favourite biblical verses of the modern retreat movement is Psalm 46:10,

> Be still, and know that I am God.

It is normally used as a call to silence, stillness and to prayer. We are to be still as to words, as to actions and outward behaviour and as to the inward frame of our hearts. This is right and true. However, its use in the psalm is rather different. The psalmist has previously called upon fellow Israelites to

> Come and see the works of the LORD,
> the desolations he has brought on the earth.

They are to be still in order to know that their God is the true and living God and that he reigns supreme both in history and among the nations of mankind. Thus the whole of verse 10 is:

> Be still, and know that I am God;
> I will be exalted among the nations,
> I will be exalted in the earth.

It is a call to meditation upon God's presence and actions in the history of nations, as well as to celebrate his final triumph at the end of the age when all peoples will bow before him. In the Old Testament this type of reflection was appropriate because all God's believing people were in one nation and thus meditation upon the state of that nation and of God's dealing with it was both possible and desirable. The inspired prophets often gave guidance in their oracles how this prayerful thinking was to progress. The equivalent today is not to meditate on world history but rather on the history of the Church of God which has branches and parts in most nations. This form of meditation is, however, for the mature in spirituality as well as the well-informed. I would not recommend it for the average Christian – better she or he keeps to providence in personal, family and local church life. Such occasions as births, birthdays, weddings, funerals, anniversaries and so on provide the raw material from which meditation can easily begin.

3. *"This is the day the LORD has made; let us rejoice and be glad in it"* (Psalm 118:24). The Lord's Day, the day when Christians meet together to celebrate the resurrection of the Lord Jesus and by word, sacrament and fellowship magnify the name of the Lord, is a day which lends itself especially to meditation. There is a powerful process of secularization going on in western culture and it is affecting the way Christians regard the Lord's Day.

Opportunities for meditation have regrettably taken second place to the reading of the fat Sunday newspapers and to the pursuit of the ever-growing number of leisure pursuits. It is of course a matter of priorities and balance which each Christian has to work out in his/her conscience. As a minimum there ought to be a time for meditation before attending Christian worship – either at home or in church (despite the regrettable talking that occurs in most congregations). Then, within the service the habit of meditating upon the scripture lessons (in the silence which follows their reading), upon the contents of the hymns as sung, the prayers as said, and the sermon as heard ought to be developed – not all at once but gradually. While receiving holy communion there is ample time to dwell in mind/heart upon some aspect of our Lord's sacrificial love and vicarious atonement. Further, at the end of worship it is good to be quiet for a while and gather together one's thoughts and feelings – even to make, as it were a spiritual bouquet to take away as we go forth to serve the Lord in his world.

FROM A FULL MIND AND HEART

Occasional meditation in the context of the natural relies upon what the senses can supply by way of information and what the memory can supply by way of received teaching and truth. Thus this discipline can be enriched through both the training of the senses to be more observant – e.g. the eyes to notice and the ears to hear – and the training of the mind to remember the great themes and teaching of Holy Scripture, the Creeds and the Liturgy. The more that is seen/heard/felt/smelt in any given situation then the more raw material there is for meditation; and the more that is understood of the principles and content of God's revelation to us then the more spiritual food can be created for the soul to digest.

To be encountered by God's revelation in and through nature it is not necessary to go further than a city park or the garden of a suburban house. There is much to behold in the flowers, the grass, the trees, the changing seasons, and so on. Of course away from the density of housing in a forest or upon a lake or in a meadow there is a larger scope for the mind to work upon. It is perhaps best to make small beginnings and to begin where you are – even with the contents of the window box outside an apartment or the potted plants inside the condominium. The mind has to be trained to get into the habit and art of occasional meditation.

Reflection upon divine providence draws heavily upon the memory both for the recalling of the events of daily life and the doctrine of God's control of our lives. This can be done in any place where there is a modicum of uninterrupted time. We can meditate in planes, on trains and in buses; while waiting for appointments and sitting on a park bench.

The pattern of individual, occasional meditations is a very personal matter and admits of few rules. A particular meditation may result only in one clear thought – e.g.

meditating on illness I may conclude that: "Every sickness is a little death. I will be content to die often that I may die once well". Or a meditation upon the created order may leave me with a great sense of delight and joy in being a part of this creation and yet made in the image and after the likeness of God. And I may conclude that: "I will enjoy all things in God, and God in all things; nothing in itself; so shall my joys neither change nor perish".

Perhaps the more we learn to meditate fruitfully in Christian worship, the more we shall be able to meditate from time to time and here and there during the rest of the week.

8
Towards a Method

Meditation upon God's revelation by members of the Body of Christ has been a constant prayerful activity from the birth of the Church to the present day. The writings of the bishops and teachers for the first seven centuries and more reveal that they had absorbed the Word of God not only into their heads but also in their hearts. Further, the rules for the common life of monasteries and convents include time for both the hearing and the reading of the Word of God and for individual reflecting upon it, by calling it to mind from memory.

However, specific methods of fixed meditation, utilizing a basic pyschology of the relation of the understanding, memory, imagination, emotions/affections and will came to the fore and were taught only from the latter part of the medieval period. For some people these proved to be a great spiritual help (especially when guided by wise pastors) but to others they seemed to be a barrier to the path of true prayer – as Teresa of Avila testified.

For those who wish to look at the developed forms of meditation in the Catholic tradition after St Teresa's time then I commend *The Art of Mental Prayer* by Bede Frost (1931). He describes the Ignatian, Franciscan, Carmelite, Salesian, Liguorian and Oratorian ways. The English Protestant tradition of the seventeenth century is now also well covered by Simon Chan, *Meditating, Puritan-style* (Cambridge University Press, 1990).

WHY UNPOPULARITY?

It seems to be the case today that not a few who adopt a developed method of regular, fixed meditation – be it a Catholic or Protestant one – find it tough going and apparently of little benefit spiritually. Why this is so is not easy to ascertain. There is obviously not any one single cause but a series of interlocking causes which form different combinations from one person to another. I mention only three of what I judge to be the major causes.

First, I believe that many who begin the art of meditation on Scripture do not first of all learn to slow down and learn to read the Bible slowly and then formatively. They are launched, or launch themselves, into what seems perhaps an artificial method before they have learned to read the Bible formatively. In other words, their souls are not sufficiently slowed down and prepared to hear and receive the living Word through a method which utilizes the various faculties/aspects of the soul. Perhaps we need to recall that the classic methods were "invented" at a time when reading was just becoming a normal activity: the printed book had not long been available. People were still aware of the great privilege of being able to read the printed word and thus they possibly read it more carefully and less quickly than we do. And, of course, they lived at a time when the pace of life was less hectic and when people were not conditioned by their culture to expect instant results and success from their activity!

In the second place, I believe that people are encouraged to seek to begin what is often called "contemplative prayer" before they have learned to meditate upon God's Word. They learn, for example, of the experience of St

Teresa of Avila (whose fascinating books today are enjoying some popularity in English-speaking countries, among Protestants as well as Catholics). She found that the methodical type of meditation (emphasizing discursive thinking, deductive reasoning and imaginative representations) which she was required to follow for many years proved totally dissatisfying as well as spiritually barren to her. However, in her case she persevered and by God's grace later discovered – quite apart from this methodical meditation – depths of prayer and communion with God which delighted her soul and which she has, in part, described in her books. So a surface reading of what she wrote can (and has) unfortunately given readers the impression that what is really important is contemplative prayer; and, in contrast, meditation is a dull and secondary kind of duty/experience. In fact (as Louis Bouyer explains so well in his *Introduction to Spirituality*, 1961, pp.68ff.), we can say that had St Teresa not lived in the worst period of the Spanish Inquisition and, further, had she been given open access to the reading of Scripture in her native language in that encounter with God known as the *lectio divina* (for which see below) her whole attitude to meditation would most probably have been very different. Her longing to know God would have been satisfied and deepened by the slow, loving and formative reading of the living Word of God. Further, her teaching on prayer would have taken meditation upon Scripture more seriously, and presented it as a genuine and divinely-ordained path into true contemplation.

So it is my belief that those who use St Teresa's books – e.g. *The Interior Castle* – to guide retreatants in prayer ought perhaps to look at the type of meditation (e.g. in the

spiritual exercises of Garcia de Cisneros) she found tor-
tuous before they allow modern Christians to think that
meditation is inferior to contemplative prayer. Formative
reading as meditation is something St Teresa missed out on
and – from heaven – now (I believe) encourages!

Thirdly, the way that the Bible is studied today, both in
the academic world and in church colleges/courses, does
not directly encourage the practice of meditation. In fact, it
probably discourages it (we shall return to this topic below
in chapter fifteen). Either formative reading or a traditional, seventeenth-century method of meditation appears
– on the surface at least – to many younger people to be
out of line with the received methods of modern, "scientific" scriptural study, and even old-fashioned and
artificial.

I want to suggest that any method used in biblical
meditation ought to be of such a nature that it is only a
developed type of formative reading. Put another way, a
sound method of meditation ought to help the reader hear,
see, taste and feel the Word of God. And, let us be clear,
this was why methods were invented at the time of the
Renaissance and Reformation (15th-17th centuries). The
methods were an ingenious exploitation of the various
resources of human psychology and sought to engage the
memory, intellect, emotions and will in appropriate ways
in order to gain a right and in-depth response to God's
revelation, written in Scripture and summarized in the
Creed. Perhaps no spiritual director was as successful as
Ignatius of Loyola in the developing of such a method. We
shall look below at one method he taught; but, first, we
shall describe the practice of what may be called basic
meditation used for centuries in the monasteries and

convents of Europe. The reader will note its similarity with what we have been calling "formative reading".

THE *LECTIO DIVINA*

Originally, in the patristic and early medieval period, *lectio divina*, divine reading, did not refer to an activity but to an object – the *sacra pagina*, the sacred page of Scripture, which is *divina* for it comes from God. However, though the divine word offers itself to us in writing, it does not cease to be and remain a word to be listened to. We can so easily forget the role of the ear in the reading of a text before the printed presses revolutionized reading in the sixteenth century. Even in private reading the words were carefully pronounced so that not only the eyes but also the mouth and ears were in action. Thus like chanting and writing, the *lectio divina*, engaged the whole body.

Of course the Bible was read and heard in the liturgy and this was regarded as of great importance not least for the development of personal spirituality. This was a *lectio continua*, the systematic and continuous reading of the Bible and the chanting of the psalms. Separated from this in time but not in ethos was the personal reading aloud quietly and slowly of the Word in the set periods for private prayer. This practice was known in monasteries as the *lectio divina*, and it gained its context and its under-girding from the corporate worship and public reading/hearing of the sacred scriptures.

The reading, *lectio*, is never seen in isolation and not done for its own sake – e.g. to gain information or knowledge. Rather, the Word is prayerfully read as the means of a spiritual encounter with the Lord. Its words are the words of salvation, addressed by God to the reader, and each word, as it were, awaits a response.

Thus *meditatio* (meditation) is the necessary prolongation of *lectio* (careful reading). Here meditating means attaching oneself firmly to the sentence one reads, weighing every word, and thereby arriving at the meaning. The meaning is gained or assimilated by reflection but also by the act of carefully pronouncing the words – the muscular exercise of the mouth. Thus the oft-used analogies of mastication, chewing the cud, and the work of the honey bee extracting the pollen from the flower. Thus *lectio* and *meditatio* are as inseparable as the physical eating and digesting of food.

The result of such *meditatio*, or better, its fruit is prayer and communion with God – *oratio* and *contemplatio*. The word that has entered the soul from the Father through the Son returns to the Father through the Son in praise and prayer. Further, the encounter with the living Christ at the heart of the Word creates the inner desire to imitate him and so leads to moral transformation. Scripture is therefore both a mirror of Christ and through him of God and also a mirror of ourselves as we are before God himself. Each of us recognizes himself in Scripture and asks himself whether he conforms to its ideal pattern.

There is a renewed interest in *lectio divina* today both inside and outside the monastic movement. It is, of course, not unlike "formative reading", described above in chapter five. What, however, needs to be borne in mind for any revival of this method is that those who engaged in *lectio divina* were the very same people who engaged in the daily offices of the monastery and gained over the years a very expansive knowledge of the contents of Scripture and Creed and were thus able to make all kinds of "divine" connections in their own minds when they read the Bible privately. I believe that the success of *lectio divina* (from the human standpoint) is the accumulated and accumulating knowledge of God's character and will, which is gained from the *lectio continua* (the continuous, daily reading of Scripture) and participation in the daily chanting of psalms, canticles, creed and prayers. In other words, the revival of the *lectio divina* is dependent upon the reverent use of the *lectio continua*.

For laity not living within a Christian community where there is a *lectio continua* the practice of *lectio divina* in a strict sense is probably impossible. The nearest is formative reading, which is itself related to the wider context of regular worship and reading of the sacred Scriptures. And this can be intensified by the use of a method of meditation – chosen carefully, possibly with the help of a wise pastor. This could be one or another of the classical methods, suitably adapted, or even one that made use of a commentary upon the text.

CLASSICAL METHODS

It became the task of Ignatius of Loyola, founder of the Society of Jesus, to adjust some of the methods current in the sixteenth century to create what has come to be called the Ignatian method. He had his own reasons for his creative revision of current methods – e.g. to test the vocation of those offering to become members of the Society. However, the method has been used over the centuries both inside and outside the Jesuit Order. It is elaborate but for those who are able to use it (again with the advice of a wise pastor, preferably a wise Jesuit) this method may be described as a finely adjusted method of meditation. At the risk of making what can be a moving experience seem dull, here it is in outline.

1. *Preliminary Preparation.* This is done the night before. The subject/text from the Gospels is chosen and carefully looked over.

The last thought before going to sleep should be on the subject.

2. *Introduction on rising.* The mind and heart to be lifted to God in acts of adoration; in the imagination the Gospel scene to be pictured and the mind fixed upon Jesus himself.

3. *The meditation proper.* Spiritual preparation is made – adoration, contrition and an offering of self to God.

(a) The first prelude: briefly calling to mind the subject and points chosen.

(b) The second prelude: seeing the place and going there in the imagination in order to be present to see, hear, touch, feel and smell.

(c) The third prelude: asking God for an interior, supernatural knowledge of our Lord; that I may love him more dearly; that I may follow him more nearly.

4. *The body of the meditation.* This consists of the application of the memory, understanding and will to the subject. The memory brings forward the subject and, as it were, hands it over to the understanding which reflects upon it, enters into it, looks at it from this angle and that, all the time seeking the meaning which it has for me.

I may ask such questions as: In the light of this what shall I do from today onwards? What obstacles shall I encounter and how should I meet them?

While his consideration is occurring my will is turning to God in acts of commitment and virtue (faith, hope, charity, humility) and I am led to make a resolution to do this or that for the Lord as a result of this meditation. The latter is made as my heart fervently pours out its petitions and desires to God our Father, to our Lord Jesus Christ and to Mary, the Mother of our Lord.

5. *The closing of the meditation.* This is not to be done abruptly but is to be made up of about fifteen minutes of quiet reflection, looking back over the meditation to see where I can improve next time.

Even where there is goodwill, courage and commitment this method demands not only much time but also a quiet place first thing on a morning. It employs all the powers of the soul and can still be beneficially used by those whose lives can be made to provide space and time for it.

There are, of course, simpler methods based on the full Ignatian method. One is easy to remember because all its parts are described by a word whose first letter is "P":

(1) *Prepare.* Become aware of God's presence with you. Find a quiet place and make yourself comfortable. Open your Bible at the passage from the Gospels you are going to meditate upon.

(2) *Picture.* Having read the incident involving Jesus picture the scene in your mind's eye: place yourself there as a participant or a keen observer.

(3) *Ponder.* Consider what you have heard Jesus say or what you have seen him do. What message does this have for you? Can you learn from the attitude of people around him?

(4) *Pray.* Convert your reflections, considerations and

thinking into prayers of desire, love and commitment and of petitions for God's help, guidance and blessing.

(5) *Practice*. Make a resolution to take into your daily living that which you recognized as being God's will through your pondering and praying.

In my *Meditating upon God's Word* (DLT 1988), I have given two further reasonably simple methods of biblical meditation. One of these makes use of a Commentary upon the text. What most of the tried and tested methods do is to use a psychological technique to help the meditator actually read the text of Scripture in such a way as it is the Word of God for and to her/him. It is, of course, very important that the method is always a servant and never the master. Further, it is also paramount that the meditator learns to read prayerfully, slowly and formatively before he moves on to any developed method of meditation. It is better to stay with formative reading than to move on to, and then get lost in, an involved meditative method.

Meditation upon sacred Scripture is most productive of spiritual benefits when undertaken daily – if not first thing in the morning then at a regular time in the day. What we have called occasional meditation – a short period of mental prayer at any time of day and night – is of course, a supplement to and not a substitute for stated or fixed meditation. Further, the call to "pray without ceasing" is the general stream of which fixed and occasional meditation may be called the rapids!

Getting started on regular meditation often occurs while on a retreat, or by becoming a member of small prayer/meditation group in a parish, or by consulting a wise pastor or experienced spiritual director, or simply by a personal decision to begin right away.

PART THREE

What is involved

9
Relaxing

In this section we shall ask ourselves what is actually involved in Christian meditation. That is how do I as a total person, a complete human being, function in the activity of meditating? To get this question in perspective we need to recall how Christians have thought about "man", the human being, as a creature before God. We need to know what kind of creatures we are and of what we are composed to order to give a right answer.

WHAT AM I?

Over the centuries there have been two dominant ways in the Church of describing a human person. One states that he is composed of body and soul, and then goes on to speak of the soul as having various faculties/aspects/ dimensions such as intellect, emotions and will. The other states that he is composed of body, soul and spirit, seeing the latter as the invisible "link" between God and the soul. Each view insists that a human being is a unity: one living person with two (or three) aspects and not two halves (or three thirds) joined together. The difference between them concerns whether God (in his good pleasure as sovereign Lord) is seen as making contact with any part/dimension/ faculty of the one, whole soul, or as communicating specifically through "spirit" to soul and body. This second approach has always been widely held in the Greek/ Russian Orthodox Church while the first has been the general view in the Roman Catholic and Protestant Churches. However, in the West there are those who take the prayer of St Paul in 1 Thessalonians 5:23 to indicate that "spirit, soul and body" do make up the triple, human identity.

We do not need to take one side or the other here since each view allows for the communion of God with the individual and the communion of the individual with God. What we need to insist upon is that the human person is a unity of body and soul (or body, soul and spirit). As such he is affected by sin and as such he will be redeemed. God does not merely save the soul but the whole person as body, soul (and spirit); heaven will be populated not by invisible souls but by the redeemed in their resurrection bodies of glory – bodies like that of the Lord Jesus who rose bodily from the dead.

If it be the case that salvation is not of souls but of believing people who also have bodies, then we must recognize that the body, which on earth is the temple of the indwelling Spirit of Christ, cannot be dismissed as irrelevant in the field of spirituality. Though some ancient manuals on asceticism (spiritual and moral disciplines) can be read as if they were saying that the body is nothing while the soul is all, and that the body must be forced into submission so that the soul may be free to commune with God, we are very aware these days of what is termed psychosomatic unity. If I worry then sooner or later my body will be affected by high blood pressure, tiredness, headaches, and so on. If I keep my body in good shape then I feel better and am less likely to suffer certain mental/ spiritual maladies. Thus disciplines whose purpose is to lead me into communion with God must include and not exclude the body, which is also in its own proper way to be in communion with God.

Of course this has always been known by the best teachers of Christian faith and living; but, the unity of the human person needs to be stated with some emphasis today because of the complex lives we live in and around great cities where people are seemingly always wanting to do things, and to get to places, faster. This is in contrast to the basically much slower pace of life in the agrarian culture of biblical times when meditation and prayer were not apparently so great a change of activity and direction as they seem to be today for someone caught up, for example, in the rush hour of any city. In fact I used to think that the vital attraction of oriental religions or eastern religious movements in the West was their offer of a non-wordly, spiritual, supra-natural way of meditation, prayer and life. However, I think that it is nearer the truth to say that they draw people by putting at the centre of religious activity the physical body – emphasizing bodily posture, diet and bodily experience. The way to the spiritual offered in through and with the body apparently stands in contrast to the perceived western Christian way of denying or making little of the body ("put your hands together" and "kneel" only) and assuming that people can turn on immediately to the spiritual.

Therefore in looking at meditation, we need to think about the function and place of the body, the soul (intellect, imagination, emotions, the will) and the actual communion with God (however, theoretically, we say this is possible) which is the purpose of the whole exercise. For, the early chapters of Genesis teach and the Letters of Paul confirm and expand, the basic truth that we are made "in the image and after the likeness of God" and so find out true human fulfilment in enjoying and glorifying God forever.

In Psalm 63 there is much to be learned of the practice of meditation, including the unity of body and soul. It begins:

> O God, you are my God,
>   earnestly I seek you;
> my soul thirsts for you,
>   my body longs for you,
>   in a dry and weary land
>   where there is no water.

The longing expressed in these verses (and the next two) is the eagerness of a friend longing to be in touch with the One he holds dear.

PREPARING TO MEDITATE

For most of us, preparing to meditate – especially if we come to it from a busy schedule or pressurized living – will include both physical relaxation and becoming aware of the presence of God. Here we add to what was said about bodily relaxation with the aim of composing ourselves for God so as to be available to him and for him. In the following chapters of this section we shall be looking at the function of the different aspects or dimensions of the soul as they are involved in meditating.

Preparatory relaxation can include the use of breathing exercises and bodily postures and will vary according to varying needs and personalities. The purpose is to create around me and in me an atmosphere of calm and silence; in particular it is to establish harmony between body and soul (and spirit) so that nothing from my side will prevent the movement of God's Spirit towards me. It is a way of making use of means to gather myself together, to possess myself and to have control over myself so as to hand over myself to God as a living sacrifice (Rom. 12:1).

The starting point for relaxation is posture. Neither kneeling nor lying down are recommended. The simplest way is that of sitting on a firm chair with a straight back so that the feet can be placed flat on the ground and the back/neck kept straight alongside the back of the chair. The head is held up with the eyes looking forward or closed. The hands can be placed on the knees, palms down, or joined together and put on the abdomen. There are, of course, other ways but they require some practice. The most well-known are those associated with yoga: they can be certainly used without reference to the religious philosophy of (Hatha) Yoga but this is easier said than done. Without doubt these postures – be they standing, seated or horizontal positions – do bring calm and peace to the whole person and, further, make of the body a good and faithful servant, prepared to unite with the soul (and spirit) in the search for and encounter with God. For those who feel sufficiently mature in their Christian faith and wish to explore this road I commend J.-N. Dechanet OSB, *Christian Yoga* (Burns and Oates, 1960). This Benedictine is very conscious of the possible pitfalls for those who go in this direction and although first published over thirty years ago in France it is still worth reading. Other more recent books commending the use of yoga exercises are less careful in their theological undergirding of the exercises.

To exist we must breathe; but there is good breathing and bad breathing, lazy breathing and deep breathing. To breathe aright is a difficult art, a fact recognized by teachers of physical education, athletic coaches, monks on Mount Athos and eastern gurus. There is a way of breathing which appears to help the majority of people who wish to meditate and pray. In fact those who do yoga exercises will find that there is a way of breathing recommended for men and another for women, based on their different physiology. Here is a simple breathing exercise known as the Dynam method and is best done sitting on a chair:

> Sit comfortably on a chair, join your hands and place them without pressure on the abdomen, just below the sternum, roughly where the diaphragm lies. After exhaling as much air as you can from your lungs, begin to breathe in by expanding first the abdomen, then the lower part of your chest, keeping the upper part still. Finally, let the upper part of the chest expand fully. As soon as this is complete, start breathing out by pulling in first the abdomen (the part that expanded first) and finish by contracting the upper part of the trunk. Then carry out the same breathing cycle again.

This exercise done just five or six times at first has the effect gradually of slowing down the rate of breathing. Women because of their different physiology may find that a better way for them is to breathe in this way:

> Inflate the chest, raising the shoulders slightly. Then go further so that air fills the middle part of the thorax and the very base of the lungs. To breathe out, start from the top by lowering the shoulders and end by drawing in the stomach a little.

The aim here is to expand the chest and slow down the rate of breathing slightly, as the art is mastered.

Whether in its masculine or feminine form, it can be done as the first part of the preparation for becoming still and quiet, and conscious of being in the presence of the Lord. Of course if this method is used then it will not be necessary to use the Benson technique (see chapter one). It is best to view this physical activity like the washing of the hands before sitting for a meal; it is not absolutely necessary but it is helpful and good in itself. Obviously people have meditated and prayed "successfully" without first doing physical exercises; the point is that to unify body and soul the physical exercises combined with the cultivation of the sense of the presence of God serve a very useful and holy end. Having recognized this we must also recognize that there are some people who do not need such preparation for their fixed time of meditation/prayer either because their interior lives are calm and peaceful, or because their personality/psychological type is not class A (i.e. not those who always must be up and doing ten jobs at once)! Further, those who are going to seek to unify body and soul in waiting upon the Lord will need to recognize that it takes time and to give the amount of time required will mean a re-scheduling of the day!

Some meditators find it best to combine the process of relaxation of body with the beginnings of prayer. They sit in a comfortable position and begin from the soles of their feet to list each part of their bodies and as they enumerate each part they seek to stretch and relax it. The process is done in a slow and gentle manner, as passively as possible. As it is done they say something like this:

I am giving over my whole body to rest passively in God's care. I hand myself over and I freely submit to the healing love and peace of my Lord. I let go of . . . and I rest totally in him. I relax my soles, my feet, my ankles, my calves, my thighs . . .; I place all gently, trustingly and peacefully in the everlasting arms of God. Like a baby in its mother's arms I lay passively in his care.

When this is completed then comes the breathing exercise which can be done to a simple rhythm such as breathe in (while counting 1, 2 slowly), pause (while counting 1, 2 slowly), and then breathe out (counting 1, 2, 3, 4 slowly). This should be done for a couple of minutes and it can be accompanied by the saying of a short prayer which breaks into two halves, so that the first part can be said while inhaling and the second while exhaling – e.g. "O Lord . . . have mercy" or "Jesus Christ . . . my Lord and Saviour" or "Breathe on me . . . Breath of God".

Following this physical preparation, there is need to make specificaly spiritual preparation. Here the advice offered by St Francis de Sales is still valid and valuable.

FOUR POSSIBLE WAYS TO BECOME AWARE OF GOD'S PRESENCE

The first way is based on the Christian teaching that God is everywhere present in and through the created order. The psalmist expressed this truth in a memorable way:

> Where can I go from your Spirit?
>   Where can I flee from your presence?
> If I go up to the heavens, you are there;
>   if I make my bed in the depths you are there.
> If I rise on the wings of the dawn,
>   if I settle on the far side of the sea,
> even there your hand will guide me,
>   your right hand will hold me fast. (139: 7–10)

If God is everywhere then he is in this space and at this time where I am. "Surely the Lord is in the place", I say to my heart.

The second way starts from the Christian teaching that believers are temples of the Holy Spirit, that Jesus Christ dwells in their hearts by faith, and, in the language of St John, the Father and the Son come to make their abode in the human soul. If God is there silently and surely in my soul, then he is nearer to me than my own breathing.

The third way looks up in faith to heaven and sees Jesus there, at the right hand of the Father in his resurrected and glorified humanity (our humanity) and pictures him and believes him to be looking down in loving concern upon all who make space and time to come in his name to the Father in prayer. I see him by faith taking a particular interest in what I am preparing to do.

The fourth way uses the imagination to see Jesus, not in heaven but as the resurrected Master, in the very place where the meditation is to take place. I see him sitting, or kneeling or standing by me, offering his wisdom, guidance and help.

Not all these ways need be used: one of them will perphaps suffice – sometimes two or three are needed to bring our consciousness into a lively sense of being in the presence of God. Our problem is, of course, not to force God down to us but to become fully aware of his gracious presence already with us.

Relaxed in mind and body, and conscious of being with my Lord Jesus, I offer a prayer asking that this time of waiting upon him will be productive of growing closer to him and deeper in his love.

*

It is probably best to do the whole meditation sitting in a

relaxed, upright manner. However, there is no reason why a move to a kneeling position (for confession, petition, intercession) or a standing position with arms raised (for praise and thanskgiving) should not occur at the end of the meditation. To be in a hurry will make all posture a hindrance for God has chosen, it would appear, to come and speak to those who wait for him and upon him.

Find rest, O my soul, in God alone; my hope comes from him. He alone is my rock and my salvation; he is my fortress, I shall not be shaken (Psalm 62:5).

Those who hope in (wait upon) the LORD will renew their strength. They will soar on wings like eagles; they will run and not grow weary, they will walk and not be faint (Isaiah 40:31).

To meditate Christianly is to wait upon the Lord Jesus Christ, to feel his presence and the warmth of his love, to listen for his word, and to be ready to do his bidding.

10
Considering

In this and the next three chapters we shall be looking at the various activities which go into formative reading, meditation, and mental prayer. These are considering, imagining, feeling, willing and remembering. Of course, to separate them is somewhat artificial for the human mind/heart is not made up of a set of separate functions but is a marvellously complex centre of related activity. However, only in considering each aspect of the activity of meditation can we appreciate fully what kind of a spiritual discipline it is.

God has given to each of us the ability to consider – to keep in and before our minds a subject for the purpose of giving attentive thought to that topic/theme/truth. This ability can, of course, be used in a variety of ways from planning how to rob a bank to working out the practical implications of a command from God; and from thinking of how to plan a new garden to reflecting on the best way to cook dinner in the shortest time.

POSSIBLE FOR ALL

Consideration in meditation is using those powers of the mind, which we all possess, to reflect, analyse (dissect), synthesize (unite harmoniously) and draw practical conclusions. However, it is done in a prayerful spirit of dependence upon God and with the intention of loving and serving him. That which is usually considered is an aspect or part of God's revelation in Scripture (e.g. some truth from the Gospels or Epistles) or in the created order (e.g. a glorious mountain view). This deliberate and active use of the intellectual powers of the mind in Christian meditation marks it off, seemingly totally, from the eastern way of meditation wherein the active role of the intellect is denied or negated.

It is important, I think, for me to emphasize that this mental activity of considering is possible for all people: it is totally false to suggest that it is only for those with academic qualifications or with high intellectual ability. No! Considering God's revealed truth is an activity for all normal Christian people, female and male, young and old (not of course the very young!). All of us use the powers of our minds to work out the meaning and implication of everyday matters. Meditation calls for no special powers; rather the powers of the mind are particularly directed in mental prayer to God's revelation; this is done in dependence upon the gracious help and guidance of the Holy Spirit, in order to see what the divine message means for each of us in our own personal, unique, life situations. And, as is true in many walks of life, practice makes perfect! So often we find that our minds are untrained or lazy and discipline is needed to get them working efficiently for the Lord in this activity of considering what he has revealed to us and what it now means for us.

Further, consideration is certainly not undertaken merely to get satisfaction out of the exercise of the intellect. (And let us be honest with ourselves, there is a particular delight experienced when the mind has been stretched and extended in intellectual activity – e.g. working on a mathematical problem or a philosophical theme.) The aim of the exercise is to love, worship and serve God, and all intellectual delight, however acceptable, is secondary. Prayerful consideration of what God has said and done has the effect in the sincere believer of opening, as it were, a way between the mind and the heart so that the heart is moved to desire those very things which the mind recognizes as right and good and true – that is, to do the will of God in daily life and give to him the glory that is his alone, for he alone is our Saviour.

SCRIPTURAL EXAMPLES

There is plenty of encouragement within Scripture for the act of considering God's self-revelation. In the Psalter the psalmists refer to their consideration of God's creation:

> When I consider your heavens,
>   the work of your fingers,
> the moon and the stars,
>   which you have set in place,
> what is man that you are mindful of him,
>   the son of man that you care for him? (8:3)

And appropriately the psalm ends with praise:

> O LORD, our Lord,
>   how majestic is your name in all the earth!

Often the psalmist remembers and considers the meaning for faith and duty of God's mighty acts such as the Exodus:

> I will remember the deeds of the LORD;
>   yes, I will remember your miracles of long ago.
> I will meditate on all your works,
>   and consider all your mighty deeds. (77:11–12)

In Psalm 107 are four poems of thanksgiving for deliverance, joined by a refrain beginning, "Then they cried out to the Lord . . ." (vv. 6, 13, 19, 28). The psalm itself closes with this verse:

> Whoever is wise, let him heed these things,
>   and consider the great love of the LORD. (v. 43)

It is in the midst of relief from suffering that the love of God is known; but, it often seems to be the case that only those who "consider" realize this and find God's consolation.

Israelites were required by God to consider the Torah, the Law given to Moses on Mount Sinai. For the Torah was the content of the covenant into which they had entered with the God of Abraham, Isaac and Jacob. Psalm 119 is a long celebration of and meditation upon the Torah. In the second of the twenty-two stanzas, in which all the lines in Hebrew begin with the letter "Beth", not only do we encounter consideration of the Law but other related activities of the soul as well; thus we are given a fine presentation of what is involved in meditation:

> How can a young man keep his way pure?
>   By living according to your word.
> I seek you with all my heart;
>   do not let me stray from your commands.
> I have hidden your word in my heart
>   that I might not sin against you.
> Praise be to you, O LORD;
>   teach me your decrees.
> With my lips I recount
>   all the laws that come from your mouth.
> I rejoice in following your statutes
>   as one rejoices in great riches.
> I meditate on your precepts

and consider your ways.
I delight in your decrees;
I will not neglect your word. (vv. 9–16)

Here we see how meditation upon and consideration of the Word (Revelation) of the LORD is intimately bound up with a right relationship with God, whom the believer seeks with all his heart.

Jesus is recorded as inviting people to consider carefully not only what he taught (Mk 6:24; Lk 8:18) and what is written in the Scriptures (Mk 2:25; 12:10) but also what is to be seen of God's work in the created order (Lk 12:24, 27, 31). The parables were offered to people to make them consider their relationship to the kingdom of God, and to himself as the King of that kingdom. In most cases Jesus used imagination to be the door first to consideration of the nature and demands of God in his kingdom and secondly to repentance and faith. From familiar images – farmers, animals, trees, plants – Jesus taught spiritual and moral truth, offered for reflection and consideration, and leading to response in discipleship.

In the Epistle to the Hebrews there are several calls to consider what God has done in Jesus but the following is probably the most telling:

Let us fix our eyes on Jesus, the author and perfector of our faith, who for the joy set before him endured the cross, scorning its shame, and sat down at the right hand of the throne of God. Consider him who endured such opposition from sinful men, so that you will not grow weary and lose heart. (12:2–3)

The call here is to consider Jesus both before and after his exaltation into heaven.

For St Paul consideration was very important in his own meditation, theology and spirituality, as his letters abundantly show. He reflected practically upon the Old Testament, upon the death, resurrection, exaltation, session and second coming of Jesus, upon the nature of God's Church and upon the kind of life into which a Christian is called. And he invited, urged and exhorted his readers to join him in this enterprise. For example, in the first of his Letters (in the order they are printed in the NT) we find in the first chapter that we are quickly led to consider what makes the Gospel so effective (Rom. 1:16–17) and what key words such as faith and righteousness mean in their Christian context.

Finally, we must not neglect to note what that most practical of apostles had to say about considering God's truth and grace. James opened his Letter with these words: "Consider it pure joy, my brothers, whenever you face trials of many kinds, because you know that the testing of your faith develops perseverance" (1:2). Later, in a very practical vein he shows how consideration can be used in self-examination: "Consider what a great forest is set on fire by a small spark. The tongue also is a fire . . ." (3:5). Finally, he points to the value of considering the lives of the saints: "As you know we consider blessed those who have persevered" (5:11).

FORMS OF CONSIDERATION

The actual spiritual/mental exercise of considering can take any one of several possible forms. For the beginner it is probably advisable first to read a passage from a Gospel in a formative way – a slow, prayerful reading (which could well involve the imaginative reconstruction of the scene involving Jesus). Then the consideration could form the answering of specific questions such as: What is the lesson I am being taught here? How does it apply to me in my particular circumstances? What reasons can I offer to convince myself that it is necessary, right and desirable that I put it into practice in my own life?

Let us assume that the passage is a part of the Sermon on the Mount where our Lord instructs his disciples: "Be perfect as your heavenly Father is perfect" (Matt. 5:48). My attempt to consider could go like this – "I recognize that the Lord Jesus is calling me to take my discipleship seriously and to be satisfied with nothing short of genuine maturity in love and holiness, purity and compassion. This means that I have to reveal spiritual and moral maturity in all aspects of my life – at home, at work, in leisure. But I realize that it is easier said than done. My mind recognizes the high standard to which I am called but my will is weak. So I must provide for myself a series of considerations to encourage myself to aim continually for this maturity/ perfection. It is my heavenly Father who calls me to imitate and share in his own perfection; it is the Lord Jesus who has set me the example of this perfection in human flesh; it is the Holy Spirit sent to me by the Father and the Son who longs to assist me to fulfill this vocation; to do the will of God is much superior to trying to please a fellow human being; I have the example of the saints and martyrs to be inspired by, and, surely, was I not born in order to enjoy and glorify God forever?" Such consideration ought to lead the meditator on to appropriate acts of will, resolution and prayer (on which see further chapter twelve below) to do God's holy will.

Another way to employ consideration in meditation is

113

through a theological theme, arising from reading the Bible, reciting the Creed, taking part in divine service or some other activity. Martin Luther was keen to emphasize this and it is prominent in his little book to which we have already made reference – his *A Simple Way to Pray* (1535). The German evangelical reformer takes each part of the Creed, Ten Commandments and Lord's Prayer as appropriate starters for meditation and prayer for his barber. Luther saw the use of God's truth in this way to be "flint and tinder" to strike "fire in the heart" of the meditator!

Eighty or so years later, Francis de Sales recommended for beginners ten basic themes for consideration in meditation on successive days. For these ten themes he supplied his own guidelines (as Luther also had done) in the hope that the reader would learn from them what considering was all about and also use them as a stepping stone into more personalized considerations. It is interesting to note that in them he uses both the imagination (see chapter eleven) and the soliloquy (see chapter twelve) within his descriptions of the required consideration. The first, and shortest, of them is on Creation.

1. Consider that only so many years ago you were not in the world and that you had as yet no being. Where was I then, O my soul? The world had already lasted so many ages, and I had not been heard of.

2. God caused you to come forth out of this nothingness, to make you what you are; having no need of you at all, except of his own goodness.

3. Consider the nature which God has given you, for it is the highest in the visible world, capable of eternal life,

and of being perfectly united with the Lord.
(*An Introduction to the Devout Life*, ed. P. Toon, 1988, p.34)

We would possibly express these three themes rather differently today in the light of the growth of science since the seventeenth century. However such (older or newer) considerations are intended to lead on to the inflaming of the heart, appropriate attitudes, acts of will, resolutions and prayer. They do this, as it were, by sending appropriate and convincing messages from the intellect to the affections and the will.

In fact each of the ten guided meditations for beginners follows the same pattern. Preparation; Considerations; Affections and Resolutions; Conclusion. The themes covered include the grace of God, human sinfulness; death, hell, heaven; and the Last Judgement. The considerations serve to take basic Christian teaching from the head to the heart and from the heart through the will into daily life as the foundation of holy living.

Of course, it is possible, to consider not only the contents of the sacred Scriptures and basic doctrines of the Creed but also the created order as personally experienced, the divine providence as it orders and relates to one's own life, and one's own self in terms of how one has behaved during a day or in particular circumstances. Such mental activity is not always easy – perhaps it is never easy; but, if undertaken in the presence of God and with the intention of serving him then the testimony of the faithful from all walks of life is that it is an excellent way into genuine prayer and Christian living. What it does is to unite the mind and heart (which often seem to pull in different directions) in their common task of serving the Lord.

Consideration is certainly an essential element in meditation. While it is not a necessary part of prayer, it is a necessary part of the careful, sincere, formative reading (or hearing) of the Word of God. It is a well-tried way of beginning the extracting of the food which God has prepared for us from the divine package in which it comes – which, as we have seen is primarily in Scripture but may also be in Sacrament, Creed, Nature or Providence. While the use of the imagination may help to set the context for, as well as to lubricate the process of consideration, it can never replace it. In fact it is doubtful whether there can be genuine meditation which does not have within it some considering, however brief, of God's revelation/word/will.

11
Imagining

Each of us has that power of the mind we call the imagination; yet some of us are more imaginative than others. Further, to be called "imaginative" may be a compliment or a criticism, depending on the source of the comment. We are particularly aware of having used the imagination when we recall a vivid dream or when we have told an exciting fairy tale to an attentive child. But in fact we use the imagination all the time: it functions alongside and in our intellect and memory. Unless we stop to analyse our thinking we would not be particularly aware of having used the imagination in this way where it is basically the servant of reason.

MAKING IMAGES

Imagination has to do with images. For example I can imagine the tree that I want to grow in my garden. By bringing together images from a variety of sources I can imagine a tree which has all the colours of the rainbow on its trunk, branches and leaves, keeps all its leaves in winter, has a nest in every branch, is one hundred metres high, and which produces fruit for Christmas which are in the shape of a Christmas pudding. In contrast to other ways of knowing – e.g. by observation – the imagination is wild and free. In fact it can seem to be both fantastical and irresponsible, the equivalent of fantasy and fancy. It was no accident that Plato, the Greek philosopher, would not have the poets, the image-makers, the fantasy-wavers in his well-ordered community (*Republic*, Bk 10). Not a few others have followed him in being wary of the powers of the unfettered imagination.

We may say that the imagination enables us to bring home to ourselves the reality of some past experience (e.g. confirmation, first communion), or grasp more intensely some experience of the moment (e.g. waiting on God for guidance), or taste beforehand in some degree an event yet to be experienced (e.g. a marriage; an ordination). The imagination is essentially realistic but, as we have noted, it can transform itself into mere fancy. By means of it we can enter more fully into the subject of our meditation, both in regard to what is being considered or desired or resolved as a result of the act of mental prayer (e.g. the picturing of virtues and values aimed at and being realized in our lives, and of people to whom we intend to act in a specific way to fulfil the vocation to serve our neighbour).

Perhaps one further word is necessary at this stage. It would appear that the imagination of some people is mainly pictorial, a capacity for realizing/creating the scene as a picture before the eyes (e.g. of the baptism of Jesus by John in the Jordan). Others find this difficult but are able to enter intensely into the feelings of the "actors" in the scene (e.g. how John the Baptist felt when required to baptize Jesus). Perhaps some people have both capacities and are able to use them both fruitfully. Our particular interest is the function – if any – of the imagination in meditation/prayer. Before we can make a positive case for, and illustrate, its use we must note the objections which have been raised, particularly within Protestantism.

OBJECTIONS TO THE USE OF IMAGINATION

We begin with the Bible, and the translation we call either the Authorised Version (AV) or the King James' Version (KJV). The first and second occurrences of the word in the book of Genesis set the scene. "God saw that the wickedness of man was great in the earth, and that every imagination of the thoughts of his heart was only evil continually" (6:5); "The imagination of man's heart is evil from his youth" (8:21; cf. also Prov. 6:18; 12:20; Jer. 23:17). We meet the same situation in the New Testament. Paul describes how the heathen are under God's wrath "because that then they knew God, they glorified him not as God, neither were they thankful; but became vain in their imaginations, and their foolish heart was darkened" (Rom. 1:21; cf. also 2 Cor. 10:5; Acts 4:25). (It is interesting to note that the New International Version (NIV), popular with modern evangelical Protestants, does not use "imagination" in any of these verses.)

When this negative use of the imagination in the KJV/ AV is combined with the doctrine that we are all sinners then there is an apparently potent reason for distrusting the use of the imagination in meditation/prayer. In fact Protestant teaching affirms that sin has not only affected the whole mind, giving it a bias towards the rejecting of God as the Lord God, but also (via the devil's temptations) can run riot in the imagination (which is naturally wild and free) causing it to make evil images, and creating sinful desires. Having said this we must also note that the word "imagination" is used in old English both as short-hand for the cogitations of unregenerate sinners (as in AV/KJV and the book by William Perkins, *Treatise of Man's*

Imagination (1600)) and as the technical term in faculty psychology for the power of the mind to make images. The two have often been confused and this has not helped the cause of those who wanted to give a positive role to the imagination.

Of course, it was also fully recognized by biblically-based Protestants that the act of spiritual regeneration (new birth) followed by the process of sanctification includes the renewal of the mind. Thus there was the possibility that the mature Christian could use the imagination fruitfully in some if not all aspects of meditation/prayer, as long as it was under the general guidance of the Holy Spirit. We shall return to this subject below.

A second reason for hesitancy about the use of the imagination in meditation/prayer was a psychological/educational one. The faculty of the imagination was deemed to be properly highly active in children; thus, with appropriate safeguards, its use was both encouraged and utilized for religious ends in the young and immature. However, the background to this reasoning was that while it is appropriate for children to be imaginative (for they have not yet reached the "age of reason"), on becoming young adults they were to learn to live according to reason, with their imagination firmly under control of that reason.

A third reason was based on practical experience. Once you encourage a person to use her/his imagination freely and without rules you have no means of controlling it. In its wild and free state it can and will lead a person to commit sins of every kind. She may see herself as a prophetess with a word to say to a sinful world. He may see himself as an apostle with power to work miracles. And so on! Thus there has developed in much modern evangelical Protestantism the active discouragement of the use of the imagination in personal Bible study for fear of possibly harmful consequences. This near prohibition relates to such activities as imagining Jesus carrying his cross to Calvary and talking to the disciples after his resurrection. Instead of using their mind's eye to picture the scene, believers have been encouraged rather to look for a practical word from the Lord in the passage under consideration about one's duty to him or to the neighbour. It is probable that this attitude is related to and strengthened by the knowledge that Roman Catholics are said to encourage imaginative mental prayer.

The fourth reason is the really important one and worthy of our close attention, even though few appear to offer it today. It was set forth with power and clarity in the seventeenth century by leading divines – e.g. Dr John Owen, whose biography I wrote under the title *God's Statesman* (1973). This objection has to do particularly with the making of images in the human mind of any of the Three Persons of the Trinity. We see "by faith" alone into the invisible world of heaven and thus we are not to construct mental pictures of "God the Father" and "God the Holy Spirit". And, though he became incarnate and lived among us, neither are we to construct mental images of Jesus Christ, "God the Son". This is because he is no longer among us on earth but is exalted in heaven. He is in the position of authority and glory and though we know he is the Lord we do not know what he looks like as he reigns in the heavenly glory. Thus we are to think of him there through rational, prayerful consideration and in faith via concepts drawn from Scripture but not through pictures created in the imagination. For to construct images of God is to break the commandment which forbids the making of any image of the living God (Exodus 20).

IMAGINATIVE MEDITATION — WITH IGNATIUS
OF LOYOLA

Even though a positive role has always been given within Roman Catholicism to the imagination, there has never been a lack of warnings about its overuse and misuse. Further, its celebrated teachers have consistently seen imaginative meditation as being a valid but inferior (in comparison with other methods) form of mental prayer. This said, it remains the only and best way for many ordinary people to begin the art of divine meditation, and this was fully recognized by Ignatius of Loyola, whose teaching is still influential within the retreat movement today. Our task now is to notice what he taught concerning imaginative meditation (which, of course, does not stand alone in his teaching but in the context of spiritual exercises/disciplines).

The fullest use of the imagination occurs when all the five senses are involved. This is called "contemplation" by St Ignatius and means to be a spectator of some special part of our Lord's life/ministry which the memory and imagination vividly construct. It can also mean to be a spectator of hell or heaven as each of these are constructed in the imagination from what memory can supply of Christian teaching.

St Ignatius describes imaginative, mental prayer in which all the five senses are used in this way:

The first point consists in seeing in imagination the persons, and in contemplating and meditating in detail the circumstances in which they are, and then in drawing some (spiritual) fruit from what has been seen.

The second point is to hear what they are saying, or what they might say, and then, by reflecting on oneself

122

to draw some (spiritual) profit from what has been heard.

The third point is to smell the infinite fragrance, and taste the infinite sweetness of the divinity. Likewise to apply these senses to the soul and its virtues, and to all according to the person we are contemplating, and to draw (spiritual) fruit from this.

The fourth point is to apply the sense of touch, for example, by embracing and kissing the place where the persons stand or are seated, always taking care to draw some (spiritual) fruit from this.

Such contemplation/meditation is, of course, set in the context of suitable preparation for, and application of it. It never merely stands alone but is part of a larger spiritual exercise. (It is in fact the fifth contemplation of the second week of the month of exercises set out in his *Spiritual Exercises*.)

To illustrate such a method is not easy for words cannot convey adequately what the involvement of the five senses achieves. The first two points, as anyone who attempts them will find, are reasonably straightforward. Thus, if we take as our example the crucifixion of Jesus we can picture in our mind's eye what happened at Calvary when Jesus was crucified between two criminals and we can hear with our inward ears what is being said by Jesus, by the criminals and by onlookers, disciples and soldiers.

The third point is possibly more difficult to grasp but the following illustration may help. Think of the experience of walking in a lovely garden. The sight of a variety of colour and beauty and of light and shadow; the hearing of the humming of bees, songs of birds and croaking of insects; and the feeling of unity, calm and repose. The total experience is something greater, higher and more subtle than mere appreciation by the senses. For my inner self is filled with joy as my mind/heart is exalted. I know inwardly what springtime, or summer or autumn really mean. Likewise, but in a spiritual manner, the absorption of the Gospel scene through an imaginative reconstruction can have the effect upon the contemplator of making possible an experience of the living God and knowing inwardly his glory, beauty and grace. Contemplating the crucified Jesus can produce a deep sense of his holy purity, his vicarious suffering, his total, unchanging love of God and human sinners, and so on.

The fourth point is straightforward, and could involve, for example touching the foot of the cross, the ground upon which falls the precious blood of Jesus, and the hem of the garment of Mary or John. This will lead on to an appropriate response – e.g. a deep appreciation of the amazing love of Jesus or a desire to be like Mary in love and obedience.

Such a method as this will, of course, work best where some actual incident or event from the Gospels or Acts is its content. The more that the memory has retained of the actual content of the Gospels the greater will be the possibility of genuine, imaginative reconstruction. Further, this method will work well for such themes as the Four Last Things: Death, Judgment, Heaven and Hell. The more the memory has retained of biblical and theological teaching the greater, again, will be the possibility of genuine, imaginative reconstruction. However, this aspect of mental prayer will hardly be appropriate for meditation upon some of the doctrinal and ethical teaching of Jesus recorded in the Gospels (e.g. Sermon on the Mount). Having said this it is possible to picture values and virtues operative in a human life and, where petitionary prayer is concerned, it is often easy to call to mind the person's face. However, it is best to follow St Ignatius and use it for major events in the life of Jesus himself. Further, the method can be simplified so that only the first and second points are used. Finally, though it can stand alone as a valid form of meditation it will function best when used along with another form – e.g. consideration.

[Note. In my *Longing for Heaven* (Macmillan, New York, 1989) I have shown the positive use of imagining heaven via biblical symbolism.]

12
Feeling and Willing

We know from experience – often painful! – that we do a job better if we do it wholeheartedly. What is done reluctantly, half-heartedly and without commitment is often badly done – unless it is a purely mechanical action, like pressing a button. The quality of an action is determined not only by my skill and clear ideas about it, but also by my desire and willingness to do it.

LOVING MUCH

Genuine Christianity consists not in knowing much but in loving much. The first commandment is not "You shall know much about the Bible and theology", but "You shall love the Lord your God with all your heart and soul and mind and strength", which is quickly followed by "And you shall love your neighbour as you love yourself". It is possible to have the clearest ideas about what ought to be done – our duty towards God – and yet be unable to get on with the doing of it. Our best actions are those in which the mind, heart and will act in unison and what we do we do whole-mindedly, whole heartedly and whole-willingly.

In terms of doing what is right we need to know in our minds what it is we ought to do, to desire in our hearts to do what we ought to do, and then have the will to get on with the doing of our clear duty. The psychology built into the traditional methods of meditation recognizes these connexions. So meditation is a means both of learning/

knowing our duty to God and of desiring and having the will to do it. In the first place the traditional methods recognize that there is the problem of imperfect, sinful humanity and of the seeming impotency of a person to be and do what she/he knows is what God requires (see St Paul's discussion in Romans 7:7–25). Then, in the second place, steps are taken both to increase the human desire to do what God requires and to empower the will to be ready to take action.

Thus we hear not only of the use of consideration (which effectively unites the mind to the heart) but the "exercise of the affections" (e.g. love, hope, joy, courage, and desire) and the making of "acts of will" (e.g. the lifting up of the soul to God in penitence for past failure, hope of future amendment, gratitude for all he has done/is doing/ will do for us, and resignation to all he may ask of us in the future).

The human heart in its loving of God is often like a fire which is still alight but is not burning brightly. It needs to be stirred and poked in order for flames to arise and to glow with light and warmth! The human will in its loving of God is often like an uninspired director: it is dull and slow. It needs to be impregnated with zeal and commitment so that it is inspired rather than expired!

The way to increase our love for God, our hope in his future, our joy in his salvation and presence, our courage to do his will, our desire to be always in his presence and our resignation to whatever his providence shall send us, is through the exercise of our faith in what God has promised to us in our Saviour Jesus Christ and written in sacred Scripture. In considering his promises written in Scripture, I see what God has done for me in Jesus and what he is today and what he will be for me tomorrow.

Thus I believe these truths: I feel humbled because of my previous unbelief and inaction; I trust what God has said because he is God; I accept it personally, for it is given to me; I commit myself to this God whose Word is true and faithful; I thank him for what he has done for me, is to me now and will be to and for me in the future: "Lord I believe; help my unbelief!"

Whether we use a simple or a developed method of formative reading/mental prayer we must include as part of our offering to God this kindling of the heart's love for God and this inspiring of the will to do the divine will. The emotions are an important part of human life and must be cultivated and developed in the loving of God. Though we do not want to engage in sentimentalism and though we do not want to rely upon our feelings, we are nevertheless called to be fervent in our loving of God – the contents of the Psalter and the Epistles leave us in no doubt about that! So though we pray for fervour we do not depend upon it.

As a result of making acts of the will, experience teaches it is wise to include a practical resolution. This is best done in terms of a matter that can be achieved by God's grace that very day (e.g. the visiting of a neighbour) and is a part of a larger commitment (to love God by visiting the elderly and shut-ins). In fact, there is little value in making general acts of the will unless they are actually converted into specific resolutions and practical acts.

TALKING TO MYSELF!

Talking to myself can really help me in my relationship with God. Actually talking to myself could be taken as a sign of senility or of insanity! Yet it is quite a normal thing to do. When I am doing a job and get it wrong, I address myself and say: "Come on, my lad, you can do better than that!" And I try again with more dedication. Have you seen tennis players talking to themselves just before they serve, when they need to win a point or when their opponent is getting on top in the match. So addressing oneself to increase determination to succeed is common in human experience. The old world for this internal conversation is soliloquy (*solus*=sole; *loqui*=speak).

If we read the Psalter and ask how the psalmists raised their desires to the point of wanting to do the will of the Lord without hesitation and obstacles, we discover that in the context of recalling the promise of God to his covenant people, they used what has come to be called the soliloquy. That is, in approaching God in prayer a psalmist actually talked to himself; but he did so knowing that God was the careful listener to this monologue and in the belief that God would actually assist in the process of bringing the desired results – as long as they were in accord with his holy will.

Take for example the question the psalmist puts to himself twice in Psalm 42 vv.5 and 11.

> Why are you downcast, O my soul?
> Why so disturbed within me?

Here his faith reasons with his fears; his hope argues with his sorrows. He searches for the cause of his troubles and his sighs give place to songs:

> Put your hope in God,
>   for I will yet praise him,
>   my Saviour and my God.

His low spirits begin to rise as he engages in self-examination! Soon his heart will be full of praise.

Then there are the wise words addressed to himself by the psalmist in Psalm 62 v.5:

> Find rest, O my soul, in God alone;
>   my hope comes from him.
> He alone is my rock and my salvation;
>   He is my fortress, I shall not be shaken.

Believers are continually being tempted to find consolation, encouragement, hope and purpose in this or that human institution or arrangement. Yet they know that only in God is their rest and hope. Thus the psalmist seeks to persuade himself to feel and act in the light of what he knows to be the truth. And because he does so in an act of prayer he looks to God to assist him.

Finally, we may point to the oft-used words which occur in Psalms 103, 104, and 146.

> Praise the LORD, O my soul;
>   all my inmost being, praise his holy name.
> Praise the LORD, O my soul,
>   and forget not all his benefits.

It seems as if he is saying to himself: "Others bless themselves and their idols, but I want humbly with ardent affection to acknowledge the Lord my God; if for no other reason than for all his blessings to me I want to venerate, I want to magnify, and I want to praise his holy name". The rest of the psalm shows that this is just what he went on to do!

The function of the soliloquy is much the same as the function of a teacher speaking to a hesitant pupil or a mother speaking to a doubting child. It is to fortify, to uplift, to give confidence to; it is to persuade gently of that which is true and right. In the context of prayer it has the special character of being not only listened to by God himself but made effective through the presence of the divine Spirit.

Outside the sacred Scriptures, there are many fine examples of the use of soliloquy in the context of meditation and prayer. The great Augustine of Hippo has a book entitled *Soliloquies* and so has Anselm (*Monologion*). However, the choicest examples of soliloquy that I have read are in the moving book *The Saints Everlasting Rest* by Richard Baxter, the English Puritan, and in *Soliloquies: or holy self-conferences of the devout soul*, by Bishop Joseph Hall of Norwich. They use and utilize them to raise the affections of the soul to desire to be with Christ in heaven, as well as to delight to do his will on earth.

HELP FROM THE PAST

It may be helpful at this stage to return to Francis de Sales and note what he included under the heading "Affections and Resolutions" in his Meditation 1: On our Creation. This will help us to see more clearly what we are discussing. In chapter ten, we noted his "Considerations" concerning the biblical and theological truth that we are creatures, wholly dependent upon our Creator; now we note what immediately follows that section:

1. Humble yourself profoundly before God saying from your heart with the psalmist, 'O Lord I am nothing before thee; why hast thou been mindful of me to create me?' Alas, my soul, you would have had no being or existence had not God created you! Without God you are nothing.

2. Give thanks to God. 'O my great and good Creator, how am I indebted to thee, since thou hast vouchsafed to

131

take me in my nothingness, to make me, by thy mercy, what I am. What can I ever do to magnify worthily thy holy name, and render thanks for thine inestimable goodness.'

3. Be ashamed. 'Alas, my Creator, instead of uniting myself to thee by love and service, I have been rebellious through my inordinate affections, erring and straying from thee, to unite myself to sin; glorifying thy goodness no more than if thou hadst not been my Creator.'

4. Abase yourself before God. 'O, my soul, know that the Lord is your God; it is he that has made you, and not you yourself. O God I am the work of thy hands.'

5. Resolution. 'From now on I will no more take pleasure in myself, since of myself I am nothing. Of what, then, have you to boast, O dust and ashes? Yes, O nothing, of what have you to exalt yourself?'

To humble myself, therefore, I resolve to do – such and such things; to suffer – such and such disgraces; I will change my life, follow my Creator, and honour in myself that condition of being which he has given me, employing it entirely in obedience to his will, by such means as shall be taught me, and as I shall ask from my spiritual director.

(*Introduction*, p.35)

It will be noticed how he goes about the task of raising the affections and making acts of will, as well as making appropriate resolutions. Further, it is interesting to see how he uses the soliloquy (e.g. his talking to himself in Nos 1, 4 and 5) to help raise the affections.

Perhaps an example of a soliloquy will make this aspect of meditating clearer. It is No 5 in Hall's book and I have modernized the English.

If we could attain to settle in our thoughts a right conception of the Majesty of God, it would put us into the comforting exercise of all the affections that belong to the soul. For, surely, if we could conceive aright of his omnipotent power, transcending glory and incomprehensible infinity, we could not but tremble before him, and be always taken up with an adoring reverence of him: and if we could conceive his infinite goodness – both in himself and to mankind – we could not but be ravished with a fervent love to him, and should think ourselves happy that we might be allowed to love such a God: and if we could conceive of that absolute beauty of his holiness and blissful presence, we could not but be inflamed with a longing desire to enjoy such a God; and if we could grasp all these together, we could not be but both enraptured with an unspeakable joy, that we have a sure relationship to a God so holy, so good, so almighty, so glorious, and (at the same time) filled with an inexpressible grief that we should either offend him or allow ourselves to neglect for a moment the felt presence of that all sufficient and all-comprehending majesty . . . O God, let it be the main care of my life to know thee and Jesus Christ, thy Son, my Saviour, whom thou has sent. Through thy mercy I cannot fail to gain here on earth an heavenly disposition of soul and a life of eternal glory with thee, hereafter.

For Hall the considering and pondering by faith of the character and nature of God is sufficient to raise the affections so that the believer desires to forsake all sin and selfishness and be with and serve his Lord.

Perhaps the greatest book from within the Protestant fold which deals with the feelings/emotions/will in the loving, worshipping and serving God is *The Religious Affections* by Jonathan Edwards, the great American philosopher-theologian (whom we shall meet again below in chapter fourteen). His works reveal not only a great intellect but a meditative mind/heart of a Christian who knew in personal experience deep and profound communion with his God. In this particular book he establishes very convincingly that the affections (we would probably say emotions and strengths today) lie at the very centre of genuine Christian living – they are, for example, prominent in the fruit of the Holy Spirit (Gal.5:22). Thus their cultivation and right directing in and through meditation is most important.

13
Remembering

Have you ever taken the time to consider what it would be like to be alive and physically in good shape but without all or part of your memory? There are some people in this position – usually due to an accident. They do not know who they are; they cannot recognize those with whom they have lived and worked; and they are unable to recall any event in their lives, even a major one.

Obviously the possession and exercise of memory is very important for human beings in all aspects of life. The ability and capacity of the brain to store information and release it when required is something we take for granted all the time. The housewife remembers her recipe for making the cake; the schoolchild remembers the route to school and the six-times tables; the office-worker remembers the places in the filing cabinets where the minutes of the meetings are stored. And so on. Each of us can give a very long list of how we use memory from waking to sleeping – and then we may add that our memory is utilized in dreaming! We sometimes complain that we have a bad memory when we actually mean that we have an untrained memory. However, like all human powers, the memory does often begin to become less efficient when we grow old.

Since the use of memory is basic to living normally, we should expect that it is basic also to our relationship with God. In fact, mental prayer is dependent upon the memory: meditation cannot be done without remembering.

135

THE COMMAND TO REMEMBER

In the Old Testament the verb "to remember" is prominent. Not only does God himself remember Israel and his covenant with this people, but also Israel is often commanded and called to remember God, his covenant, and his mighty deeds. Even as the Lord God himself remembers, so is Israel to remember; and in each case remembering is in order to fulfil what has been promised in the covenant made between the Lord and Moses (for the tribes of Israel).

The Israelites were so often forgetful of their duty to their God; thus, all they deserved was rejection and punishment by him. Yet so often he spoke to them saying, "I will not reject them or abhor them . . . I am the LORD their God . . . I will remember the covenant with their ancestors whom I brought out of Egypt in the sight of the nations to be their God. I am the LORD" (Lev. 26:44–45). The righteous remnant within Israel realized that their very existence depended upon God's remembering of them and they prayed that he would remember the covenant he had made. Jeremiah poured out his soul to God, acknowledging the wickedness of the people and praying: "For the sake of your name do not despise us; do not dishonour your glorious throne. Remember your covenant with us and do not break it" (14:21).

One of the key words in the fifth book of Moses, Deuteronomy, is "remember". Because of who the Lord God is, what he has done, what he has said, and what has happened to the people of Israel, there is much to call to mind in order to reflect upon and live by. Further, events of the past are to be called to mind in such a way as what they signify becomes a reality to those who remember.

Remembrance bridges the past and present without losing the distinction between them. It is a pattern of historical understanding and Hebrew/Jewish life had a pattern of reminders (e.g. festivals, holy days) by which to remember; these challenged them to hold God in memory, and thereby to live in his presence.

Here are the first four calls to remember:

"Remember the day you stood before the LORD, your God at Horeb . . ." (4:10)

"Remember that you were slaves in Egypt and that the LORD your God brought you out of there with a mighty hand . . ." (5:15)

"Remember well what the LORD your God did to Pharaoh and to all Egypt" (7:18)

"Remember how the LORD your God led you all the way in the desert these forty years, to humble you and to test you in order to know what was in your heart . . ." (8:2)

We can trace the call to remember through the books of the Old Testament via the psalms (where the verb "to remember" occurs frequently) through to the last reference in Malachi where the people are commanded by the prophet: "Remember the law of my servant Moses, the decrees and laws I gave to him at Horeb for all Israel" (4:4). Of course the great festivals (the weekly Sabbath and the annual feasts of Passover, Pentecost, Trumpets, Day of Atonement and Tabernacles) described in Leviticus 23 were periods of time when what God had done and said were recalled in order to know and affirm his continuing covenant with them and their commitment to him. Memory forms a kind of bridge, within the ongoing tradition of worship and obedience, linking the past and

137

present; and it does do in a dynamic way. Therefore the recalling of the events is also the affirming and experiencing of the God who never changes and who is Lord of history.

The occurrence of the verb "to remember" is less common in the New Testament; but it is used in the very important passage which describes the institution by Jesus of the Lord's Supper – "Do this in remembrance of me" (Lk. 22:19; 1 Cor. 11:24–25). We shall return to the theme of remembering and meditating in worship in Part 4. It is also associated with prayer: "We continually remember before our God and Father your work produced by faith . . ." (1 Thess. 1:3); and with believing and confessing the Faith: "Remember Jesus Christ, raised from the dead, descended from David" (2 Tim. 2:8).

Of course both the Old Testament and New Testament belong to a period of human history when (handwritten) books/scrolls were rare and thus people committed to memory much more than we need to do today with the general availability of information of all kinds, close at hand, in written and electronic sources. They had to commit to memory what they were taught and what they learned because there was no other (easy) way of getting that information at a later date. This was so for all aspects of life from farming to fishing. It was also true of religious and moral teaching, which of course was integrated into the whole of life, personal, family and social, in Israel. So children learned at least parts of Law of Moses off by heart as well as learning various psalms to use as prayers. Thus when the prophets called upon the people to remember, they were actually asking them to recall what they had been taught and had committed to memory. Further, in examples of meditatory prayer (e.g. Psalms 19 and 119) there is a necessary emphasis on "remembering" the Law of the Lord. It is probably true to say that the religion and spirituality of the Old Testament could not make sense if the act of remembering were not an integral part of it.

DO I NEED TO REMEMBER?

We live in a civilization and culture where there is a massive availability of printed material. The Bible itself comes to us in a variety of translations, sizes, and prices. We can carry a copy everywhere in a pocket or handbag. In fact we can carry a copy which has a handy-reference within it pointing us to various themes, texts and so on. So if in need we can quickly look up an appropriate verse. Then it is possible also to obtain prayer books in a variety of sizes and prices. So we can have immediate access, by use of the index, to an appropriate prayer for every occasion. In fact we can now pick up the phone, dial a number, and hear a prayer or scripture verse!

One response to this modern availability of God's Word, and devout human response to it in prayers, would be to say this. "Since we do not need to use the memory to the extent that our ancestors did we do not need to learn God's Word off by heart." This case can be strengthened by referring to "learning by heart" by the pejorative expression "learning by rote" (meaning in a mechanical manner), and suggesting it is a rather old-fashioned practice, not favoured by leading, modern educationalists. It can be underlined further by pointing out that there are so many different translations and paraphrases of the Bible that it is hardly worthwhile seeking to memorize any particular one of them.

Another response – and I think the right one – is to

affirm and gently to insist that the need to memorize the Word of God (and possibly also important prayers and collects) is as valid today as at any time since the Israelites were first commanded to keep the Word of God in their hearts. The Word on the page is very different from the Word in the heart. The old expression "learning by heart" captures what is our duty before God. We do not learn the Word of God in parrot or mechanical fashion (although saying it over and over again may well be right in certain circumstances). We learn it by reading it over each day, slowly and prayerfully so that its real content/meaning enters our minds and hearts as digested food. (This was one theme of chapter five above.) Perhaps it is necessary to add that in our reading it is best to stay with one translation rather than using several and thereby confusing the work of memorization.

We also learn the Creed and seek to understand it so that we have in our minds a structure of understanding concerning who is our God and what he has done and will do for us and our salvation in Jesus Christ. Then, what we learn by heart from sacred Scripture both goes into this structure of understanding and becomes part of that total knowledge which is the basis of our communion and fellowship with God. We add to this learning by heart through hearing sermons, attending Bible studies, reading Christian literature and so on. We store the Word of God in memory and we do so in such a way that the store is growing in size and quality as the weeks go by.

But why do this? The answer is quite simple. We store it in memory to be able to recall it when needed; and, if we are living a faithful Christian life it is needed all the time! We need it to be able to resist the devil, to overcome temptations, to witness winsomely, to confess courageously, to pray faithfully and to meditate successfully. In all these, as well as other occasions, there is no time either to look up a reference in a book or turn on the computer and get the information required from the disk. We cannot dispense with the use of memory in the Christian life and certainly we cannot eliminate it from meditation. (In contrast it has no practical function at all in eastern meditation.)

Let us consider the practice of fixed meditation upon a passage of the Gospels or Epistles. It is from memory that we call that general background information and understanding which enables us to read the passage meaningfully and to set it in the right context. This is the case for using the imagination to reconstruct the scene – we recall what we know of, say, the geographical and cultural background to the Gospel (e.g. the layout of Jerusalem and the way people dressed); and it is also the case for the use of consideration – we recall such doctrinal and moral teaching as is particularly connected with the topic upon which we are exercising our minds (e.g. how Jesus described himself, if we are considering the identity of Jesus as our Saviour). The richer is the store of memory the richer will be our meditation, by the grace of God.

Take, also, the practice of occasional meditation. Here the recalling from memory what has been learned is of great importance in order for this short mental prayer to succeed. If, for example, the meditation is set in motion through the sight of a beautiful natural scene, then from the memory must be called forth such biblical teaching as that God is the Creator and Preserver of the universe, that this creating and preserving is through the eternal Word

141

(Son), and that this present creation is awaiting its transformation into the new order at the second coming of Jesus, Incarnate Word (Son). The more we have learned by heart concerning the theme of creation in the Bible the more we shall be able to utilize it in an occasional (as well as a fixed) meditation.

The same point can be made concerning meditation within divine worship, be that service a fixed liturgy from a Prayer Book or an *ex tempore* service in a nonconformist congregation. To meditate upon the lessons when read, the sacraments when celebrated and the sermon when heard requires the calling to mind of appropriately related truth, information and facts from the memory. And, again, the more that is stored, then the richer can be the meditation offered to God.

I shall make one last point. This arises from my visiting, as a pastor, older people who are sick and perhaps near to the end of their earthly pilgrimage. I am impressed by their ability to recall from memory passages of the Bible, answers in the Catechism, familiar Collects from prayerbooks, and verses from psalms and hymns. They are able to recall these and to make them their prayers – often their simple, meditative prayers. I do not want to say that how we pray on our death-beds will determine where we spend eternity; but I do want to say that if our memory is well stored with the Word of God and devout responses to that Word (in Collects, hymns etc) then we shall have a greater potential for comfort, hope, faith, love and prayer as we draw near to the gate which opens into the next life and into the possibility of the beatific vision of God.

To summarize: there is no substitute in Christian spirituality for the learning by heart of the essential doctrines of the Creed, the basic content of the Gospel of God concerning

Jesus Christ, and the outlines of the apostolic faith and teaching concerning this same Jesus Christ. To neglect this duty of learning by heart is to miss out on many of the blessings which God wishes to bestow upon us.

"Lord remember me and help me to remember you."

14
Encountering

If meditation/mental prayer involves dialogue with God then there will be an encounter with God – whether we are aware of it or not. The form of the encounter will vary from a sense of being illuminated in mind concerning an aspect of divine truth to hearing God speak a definite word of encouragement or guidance with his "still, small voice" deep in the heart. It may mean having a visionary experience or entail a vital sense of being quite still and restful in the holy yet comforting presence of the living God. Some days there will be a more obvious sense of the divine presence, a richer experience of the grace of God, a clearer view of the glory of God in the face of Jesus Christ, and a deeper faith in the invisible reality of the kingdom of heaven; and other days there will be a kind of darkness and God will be there for faith to hold on to within that darkness. For true meditation or mental prayer (from *mens, mentis*, meaning heart as well as mind) involves the whole soul, with the mind descending, as it were, into the heart to know God's presence and feel his energizing of the will to walk in his ways.

PERSONAL TESTIMONY

Instead of seeking to describe the dynamic nature of true meditation upon God's truth, I shall present several testimonies from saintly Protestants. First of all, George Müller (1805–1898), a German by birth, is well-known for the orphanage he founded in Bristol (which still exists), for his living by faith and for his preaching at conventions of the Open Brethren. He has left behind a marvellous account of his own meditation and this shows its nature as a spiritual exercise (*Autobiography*, pp. 152–4).

He tells how his practice at first was to arise early on a morning and give himself immediately to prayer and seek to pray until breakfast. However, he found that his mind wandered and it seemed to take him fifteen minutes or more until he felt that he was really into the act of praying and of communicating with his Lord. Then, suddenly, it came to him one day that "the first thing that a child of God has to do morning by morning is to obtain food for the inner man"; and the food for the inner man is not in the act of praying but in the reading of the Scriptures. Yet not any kind of reading for a simple reading of the Bible leads to the content passing through the mind "just as water runs through a pipe, but considering what we read, pondering over it, and applying it to our hearts". (I find it most interesting that what Müller came to see by a sudden flash of inspiration/illumination is in fact a summary of the classic western form of meditating upon Scripture.) Later in life he often spoke warmly "of the immense spiritual profit and refreshment" he was conscious of having derived from this way of using the Scriptures.

This is how he described his early morning meditating upon what he reverently and affectionately termed "the Word of God":

Now I saw, that the most important thing I had to do was to give myself to the reading of the Word of God and to meditation on it, that thus my heart might be comforted, encouraged, warned, reproved, instructed;

and that thus, whilst meditating, my heart might be brought into experimental communion with the Lord. I began, therefore, to meditate on the New Testament, from the beginning early on a morning. The first thing I did, after having asked in a few words the Lord's blessing upon his precious Word, was to begin to meditate on the Word of God, searching as it were, into every verse, to get blessing out of it; not for the sake of the public ministry of the Word; not for the sake of preaching what I had meditated upon; but for the sake of obtaining food for my own soul.

In our terminology this is an intense, "formative" reading of the Gospels. Here is how he described the normal process and outcome of his waiting upon the Lord:

The result I have found to be invariably this, that after a very few minutes my soul has been led to confession, or to thanksgiving, or to intercession, or to supplication; so that though I did not, as it were, give myself to prayer, but to meditation, yet it turned almost immediately into prayer. When thus I have been for awhile making confession, or intercession, or supplication, or have given thanks, I go on to the next words or verse, turning it all, as I go on, into prayer for myself and for others, as the Word may lead to it; but still continually keeping before me, that food for my own soul is the object of the meditation. The result of this is, that there is always a good deal of confession, thanksgiving, supplication, or intercession mingled with my meditation, and that my inner man almost invariably is even sensibly nourished and strengthened and by breakfast time, with rare exceptions, I am in a peaceful if not a happy state of heart.

There is a very fine line – if it can be drawn at all! – between meditating and praying and Müller's testimony shows how one leads to the other and vice versa. What he describes is a series of meditations, one after the other and each one leading into one or another expression of prayer. Not all of us can spend the amount of time he did each morning in meditating and so ours must needs be a more limited if not a less real experience.

What Müller does not describe in his account of meditation is the experience of being led by the Spirit into an act of adoration in which, as it were, the whole soul is caught up in beholding the glory of God in the face of Jesus Christ: and for a while space and time are forgotten as the soul is ravished with the sight and the sense of the holy love of God. He did know this experience even as have thousands of other Christians.

Perhaps the greatest American theologian/philosopher is Jonathan Edwards (1703-1758). Not a few of his books may be described as theological meditations. In fact, he began to take Christian faith and life seriously as a result of a meditation:

The first instance, that I remember, of that sort of inward, sweet delight in God and divine things, that I have lived much in since, was on reading the words of 1 Timothy 1:17 ('Now unto the King eternal, immortal, invisible, the only wise God, be honour and glory for ever and ever. Amen.'). As I read these words there came into my soul, and was as it were diffused through it, a sense of the glory of the Divine Being; a new sense, quite different from anything I had ever experienced before. Never any words of Scripture seemed to me as these words did. I thought with myself, how excellent a Being

147

that was, and how happy I should be, if I might enjoy that God, and be rapt up to him in heaven, and be, as it were, swallowed up in him for ever! I kept saying, and as it were singing, over these words of Scripture to myself; and went to pray to God that I might enjoy him, and prayed in a manner quite different from what I was used to do; with a new sort of affection . . .

From about that time I began to have a new kind of apprehensions and ideas of Christ, and the work of redemption, and the glorious way of salvation by him. An inward, sweet sense of these things at times came into my heart; and my soul was led away in pleasant views and contemplations of them. And my mind was greatly engaged to spend my time in reading and meditating on Christ, on the beauty and excellence of his person, and the lovely way of salvation by free grace in him.

(Works (1829) Vol. 1., pp. 60–61)

Like Augustine and Anselm, there is in Edwards a brilliant mind which is totally ravished by the excellency of the nature and beauty of the living God, whom he longs to know both by mind and heart, intellectually as well as experientially.

A young friend of Edwards was the saintly young man, David Brainerd (1718–1747), pioneer missionary to North American Indians. He kept a *diary* of his relationship with God and work amongst the Indians, and it was published by Jonathan Edwards after his death. There are many moving accounts of his meditations and prayers, including his attempts to describe the powerful sense of the presence of God that he often felt. Here is his account of what happened after meditation on Tuesday June 15, 1742:

I could do nothing but tell my dear Lord, in a sweet calm, that he knew I longed for nothing but himself, nothing but holiness; that he had given me these desires, and he only could give me the thing desired. I never seemed to be so unhinged from myself and to be so wholly devoted to God. My heart was swallowed up in God most of the day. In the evening I had such a view of the soul being as it were enlarged, to contain more holiness, that it seemed ready to separate from my body. I then wrestled in agony for divine blessings; had my heart drawn out in prayer for some Christian friends beyond what I ever had before. I feel differently now from whatever I did under any enjoyments before; more engaged to live for God for ever, and less pleased with my own frames (dispositions).

He records under Tuesday December 21, 1742 how he entered into imageless prayer, what Roman Catholics have called unitive or contemplative prayer:

God enabled me to pray with as much spirituality and sweetness as I have done for some time; my mind seemed to be unclothed of sense and imagination, and was in a measure let into the immaterial world of spirits.

For Friday, January 6, 1744, he wrote as follows:

My soul intensely longed that the dreadful spots and stains of sin might be washed away from it. Saw something of the power and all-sufficiency of God. My soul seemed to rest on his power and grace; longed for resignation to his will, and mortification to all things here below. My mind was greatly fixed on divine things; my resolutions for a life of mortification, continual watchfulness, self-denial, seriousness, were strong and fixed; my desires ardent and intense; my conscience tender and afraid of every appearance of evil ... Time appeared very short, eternity near ...

His method of meditation was quite simple. He read slowly and prayerfully the text of Scripture, applied it to himself, and proceeded to pray as the Spirit led him.

THE VALUE OF OTHERS' EXPERIENCE

The purpose of reading what the saints – be they Protestants or Roman Catholics – have experienced is not to discourage us by making us think that we cannot attain their heights. Rather it is to show us just what is possible by the guidance and assistance of the Holy Spirit in the enjoying and the glorifying of God in our souls and in our lives.

There are of course modern examples of the importance and role of meditation. One is supplied by Dietrich Bonhoeffer, who was put to death by the Gestapo in 1944. He came to appreciate in depth the discipline of meditating upon the Holy Scriptures during the 1930s when the Church in Germany had to decide how to respond to the Nazi propaganda and pressure. One of the rules for the seminarians at Finkenwalde, where Bonoeffer was the Principal, was that they devote half an hour each morning to silent meditation upon Scripture. He prepared for their use a short and excellent paper entitled "Instructions in daily meditation". One brief section answers the question, "What do I want from my meditation?" Here is a part of his answer:

We want to rise up from our meditation in a different state from when we sat down. We want to meet Christ in his Word. We turn to the text in our desire to hear what it is that he wants to give us and teach us today through his Word. Meet him first in the day, before you meet other people . . . His fellowship, his help, his guidance for the day through his Word – that is the goal. Thus you will begin the day freshly strengthened in your faith.

He insisted that "it is necessary that there be complete quiet and that we intend to allow nothing to divert us, no matter how important it may seem".

Some of his letters and papers relating to the absolute need for meditation to accompany prayer are found in the little, admirable volume entitled *Meditating on the Word* (Cowley Publications, Cambridge, Mass., 1986).

For those who wish to approach this subject and find testimony from a traditional Catholic and Carmelite viewpoint, I would commend *In Search of God: with Teresa of Avila, John of the Cross, Thérèse of Lisieux and Edith Stein* (New City Press, NY, 1989 & Collins, 1990) by Waltraud Herbstrith (Sr Teresia a Mater Dei, OCD). She describes how Edith Stein (1891–1942) the convert from Judaism who became a Catholic and a Carmelite only to be killed in a gas chamber by the Nazis, loved her daily meditation. In a private letter she wrote: "I love the divine office and I am displeased whenever I miss the choral prayer, even that of the little hours (Mattins & Vespers), but the foundations of our life are the two hours of meditation we have in our daily agenda. Only now that I

151

enjoy this benefit do I know how much I was missing outside the convent" (p.23). Two hours is more than the average lay Christian can manage – unless she/he be retired, but it is the principle not the time that counts before God.

PART FOUR

How it develops

15
Bible Study and Meditation

We have said much about formative, meditative reading of holy Scripture and little of the study of the holy books. It is now time to affirm that there can be great value in studying the Bible at any level. The Bible is, as we all know, made up of two separate collections of books, written originally in Hebrew and Greek. Further, the books are of different kinds – e.g. collections of poems, laws and prophetic oracles, together with personal and general letters. Over the centuries the Church has taught that these books have an inner unity and constitute the written Word of God, the inspired record of and witness to God's revelation of himself to his creation.

AIDS FOR BIBLE STUDY

All the books were written long ago. Therefore an ordinary Christian can find it most helpful to study the general context from which they came – such topics as the geography of Palestine, the social and family customs of the ancient near East, the style of Hebrew poetry and prose, the symbolic language called apocalyptic (found in the Revelation of St John), the teaching method of Jesus, the meaning of the phrase "kingdom of God/heaven", and so on. She/he can also benefit greatly from a guided introduction to the history and religion of Israel, the life of Jesus,

155

the history of the early Church and the contents of the Old and New Testaments.

There is an abundance of material to help the ordinary Christian who wishes to become familiar with the general nature and contents of the Bible. Dictionaries and commentaries, concordances and lexicons, together with summaries of biblical doctrines, the teaching of Jesus and of Paul may all be easily purchased or borrowed. Thus Bible study either alone or within a group can be most interesting! It can even be quite fascinating at times! Perhaps too intriguing! Some people get wholly intrigued by the attempt to sort out the "signs of the times" while others are absorbed in the general structure and contents of the ancient tabernacle/temple.

The reason why there is an abundance of easily-accessible material is that there is at the university/college level a long tradition of academic theological and biblical study. Here people earn their living by being professional students of the Bible. The Church, of course, owes much to this tradition of scholarship. Because of it, we have translations into our language of the books of the Bible from their original Hebrew and Greek originals. Scholars who have mastered these ancient languages also provide us with the basic information from which the popular dictionaries, encyclopedias, commentaries and lexicons are produced.

However, this valuable work of scholarship does not require the person involved to be, of necessity, a Christian believer. Obviously there must be general sympathy with the religion of the Old and New Testaments; but, what is primarily required in a scholar, who works in a university, is appropriate ability and skills.

As far as I can tell, those Christian people who use the

more conservative type of biblical dictionaries, encyclopedias and commentaries find no barrier between study of the Bible and meditation upon it. In fact when things are going right the one flows into the other. Often, my own study of the Bible has become meditation upon it; further, others have told me of occasions when a church bible-study group has become a meditation/prayer group simply through paying attention to the content of sacred Scripture. This is, I think, a development inspired by the Spirit of Christ, who can turn believing, reverential study into a time of prayer.

A FELT DIFFICULTY

Though many will find the following claim difficult to take, I make it because I think it is true – academic study of the Bible can be a barrier to the true knowledge of, and communion with, God. It need not be; it ought not to be; but it can be! Centuries ago Cassian was much aware of both the benefits and the snares of study. As we see from his *Conferences* (Nine and Ten), he allowed that the mind should engage in academic studies; yet he was afraid of it, at least with younger men, because monks had noticed how easily the pursuit of academic knowledge leads to pride in knowledge and to a vanity, causing the young man to speak too quickly and show off his logic or information or whatever. Why, we may ask, was this so? Because the inner content of the Bible is most (sometimes only) accessible to the mind/heart which is spiritually prepared by penitence and prayer to receive it. Holy things have to be received in holy ways: otherwise that which is holy can become a snare. Study in which there is a search for information and insight for its own sake (not for the sake of the glorifying of God) can so easily feed imperfect, sinful human nature and thus feed pride and vanity instead of humility and holiness.

The tension between academic study of the Bible and meditation upon it recognized in the Egyptian desert by the monks did not go away. It remained through the medieval centuries as a problem to be faced by the communities in the monasteries which were often the custodians of academic learning. And it continued as a problem through the period of the Renaissance and Reformation to modern times. However, it has recently become more acute – too acute for many – with the development and popularization of modern "scientific" approaches to the study of the Bible. Put simply, those who study the Bible today in the university, college (and even in the seminary) do so according to the accepted methods of the secular academia. Not only are the books of the Bible examined as examples of ancient literature but also their contents and claims are analysed according to one or another of the dominant modern philosophical views.

The results of what used to be called "lower criticism" (i.e. literary, historical and grammatical studies) has been and can be most illuminating as the basis for supplying the general background context in which those who want to read the Bible formatively do can do so.

In contrast, that academic study ("higher criticism") which comes to the text with modern "critical" views concerning such subjects as miracles, prophecy and revelation assumes a judgemental position over against the text and attempts to sift what is regarded as the real content from the husk or shell in which it is lodged. Thus, for example, if it is assumed that God always works according to the (= our) known laws of nature then the virginal conception of Jesus, his bodily resurrection and virtually all the miracles which he and his apostles performed are denied in their literal sense. Rather they are presented as what the early Christians believed to have occurred. Further, if it is assumed that prophecy is only a forth-telling and not also a fore-telling then the way in which the psalms and prophetical books of the Old Testament are read and interpreted is very different from that reading which accepts them at their "face value". Then also, if the traditional view of revelation (God actually speaking to individuals and inspiring them to record what he wanted preserved) is set aside as being a non-scientific view, the way is open to present the contents of this or that book as "the views of St Paul" or "the ideas of Hosea" and so on, and to stand in judgment upon them. The person who has studied in this atmosphere does not always find it easy or natural or even meaningful to use the sacred text for meditatory prayer!

However, probably that which has made the beginning of formative reading or serious meditation most difficult, even impossible, for some educated Christians is the way in which the Gospels have been studied in modern times. They have been subjected to what is called in the trade form criticism, redaction criticism and structural criticism, to add to the older disciplines of literary and source criticism (for details see e.g. W. Barnes Tatum, *In Quest of Jesus: A Guidebook*, John Knox Press/SCM Press, 1983). The effects of all this upon many students – including those who become professional ministers – is to cause them to approach the text with a host of questions and problems and thus, for example, they may hesitate to attribute to Jesus any saying which is recorded in the Gospels as being said by him, or have doubts as to whether this or that miracle really occurred. Thus it is difficult, to say the least, to receive the text as Word of God for meditation upon a saying if one has come to believe or to suspect that it is adapted, developed or produced by the early Church from something Jesus said; and further that the Church might have been mistaken in its views!

As a way out of the problem, some retreat conductors encourage theological students to make a meditation upon the Gospels which is wholly imaginative and affective, with virtually no consideration. I can see that this may help in the short term but it is hardly likely to help in the long term, for it is avoiding rather than facing a problem.

TOWARDS A SOLUTION

There are various responses to this situation. One is simple: it is not to attempt to read the Bible formatively or to meditate upon it using one or another of the older methods of mental prayer. Put positively, it is to read the Bible "as a modern person" and to use it, along with other sources, as a means of learning about God, Jesus, and the Christian Faith. Not a few adopt this position today and, as far as I can tell, do so not as a thought-out approach but as a kind of reflex action to the situation they have encountered in their studies. They may also begin to use an eastern method of meditation which of course requires no use of the sacred text – except perhaps to supply a "mantra" or focus phrase.

A second response is to separate as far as possible the two activities of (a) academic study of the Bible and (b) meditation upon sacred Scripture. This may work for part of the time but it will be necessary, at least some of the time, to dismiss from the mind as "distractions" the questions raised by modern scientific criticism. If this is done too often, the meditator is in danger of becoming a split personality, unable to bring to God the content and results of the academic study!

A third response, which I would advocate, is to affirm before God that we need both reverent academic study and formative/meditative reading of Scripture. However, I would want to insist that (a) the formative reading of Scripture has priority over the academic reading/study of Scripture, and that (b) the academic study is to be seen as important background to the formative reading. I recognize that I am advocating a position which is not a common one today but I think it is necessary to advocate it in order to be faithful to Jesus Christ in our generation.

In fact I believe that this way of stating the relationship is to be preferred to a fourth response, which is widely held in moderately conservative circles in both the Roman Catholic and Protestant Churches. This is to claim that the two are of equal importance and should feed into each other, with one or the other assuming and taking the priority in different situations. In other words they are to be seen as the two sides of one coin. I wish this position were tenable today just as it was in earlier centuries when the study of the Bible was seen as a specifically Christian activity. Now, as we all know, a different ethos guides professional studies in university faculties of theology/religious studies (even though there are individuals working in them who are critical of that ethos).

In contrast to the approach to the Bible within the secular university, the Scriptures are seen within the believing Church and in historical Christianity as being like a long love letter sent from heaven to his Bride, the Church, by the Bridegroom, the exalted Lord Jesus. As

161

such they cannot be treated only in an academic way. A lover is not interested in grammar or syntax, archaeology or etymology: she is only interested in the beloved, in what he says, reveals, and promises. She savours the letter with tenderness and with expectancy. The paper is precious to her because it is that upon which the beloved has written of his love and the very touching of it, feeling it and reading it produces all kinds of inner sensations. She will recognize meanings and intimations in the words which others could never do for love has special qualities as an interpreter. (This explains why some Christians insist on carrying in their breast pocket, next to their heart, a copy of the Bible.)

Other analogies which serve to highlight the way the Bible is read by the Church as the source of meditation/ prayer are those of (a) disciples reading their most highly respected teacher's writings, and (b) soldiers reading their orders before battle.

Yet also the Church must assume at times the role of the academic investigator, grammarian, etymologist, literary critic, translator, and historian. This is a duty because the Bible is not a contemporary document but a collection of ancient documents into which most of us can only have access through translation. If the work of the Church in academic study is done humbly and from faith to faith by her "doctors" and "professors", then for most of the time it will provide a rich background to assist the reception of the Word as it is read, preached, and heard. Tensions and difficulties will no doubt regularly arise which may separate, as it were, the head from the heart, but these will be solved eventually, in the context of worship, love and faith.

The real situation today is, regrettably, that little

academic study is apparently done from faith to faith. Rather, it is done to satisfy criteria which are not set by the believing Church but by the secular world. Of course, this does not mean that all the results of academic study are of no use to the believing Church. In practice many are, but, they usually come in a parcel which contains others which are destructive of true faith. Thus, for example, great discrimination is needed by the pastor using a modern academic commentary on a book of the Bible in preparing a sermon. He may learn a lot about the different views of scholars on this or that point and not glean anything that is food for the weary, troubled, anxious, enquiring, expectant soul.

I know from experience that the attempt to combine the academic study of the Bible with meditating upon the Bible is far from easy. I do not think there is any simple advice I can give except to emphasize that only if we give the absolute priority to the daily meditation upon the text (keeping to the Psalms and Gospels and selected Epistles for the first year or more) seeking to treat it as the Bridegroom's love-letter to his Bride will we ever begin to resolve this problem. Those who do this may be criticised and called "fundamentalists" or "traditionalists" or "anti-intellectual"; but, they will over a period of time find that material from their studies is beginning to become food upon which their soul is able to feed in prayer before God. And, surely it is better to please the Lord and serve him than win any earthy acclaim or conform to the secular spirit of the world!

16
Praying the Psalms

In the last chapter we looked in general at the subject of study and meditation. Here we take a specific book of the Bible and look more closely at this relationship.

THE PSALTER

Apart from the four Gospels no biblical book has been the source of Christian meditation more than the Psalter (which itself is really five books joined together to make one). In fact the Psalter has always had a central place in both Jewish and Christian corporate worship and private prayer. Though only selected psalms were used in the Jewish synagogues, we may nevertheless affirm that the Psalter was the prayerbook of Jesus, his apostles, and the early Church. Only, however, with the arrival of monasticism in the fourth century was the practice developed of reading/reciting the whole Psalter in course. This was an individual devotion, done corporately, and in the belief that the contents of the Psalter are a microcosm of Holy Scripture. Since the patristic period, the Churches of East and West (and including the Protestant Churches) have been united in using the Psalter both for public worship and private meditation and prayer.

There is a beautiful Latin expression which captures the traditional Christian use of the psalms: *semper in ore psalmus, semper in corde Christus* (always a psalm on the

lips, always Christ in the heart). St Benedict taught monks
"so to say the psalms [at the daily office] that our heart is
in harmony with the words on our lips" (Rule 19:6).

The *Book of Common Prayer* (1552, revised 1662) of
the Church of England provides for the reading/chanting
of the psalms at both the morning and evening services of
every day of the year. In this way the whole Psalter is read/
sung (prayed) through once a month. However, in modern
Anglican prayerbooks, though the use of psalms is still a
basic part of both Morning and Evening Prayer, the
number used daily has been reduced. These are either said
or chanted according to local circumstances. In contrast, in
other Churches – e.g. the Church of Scotland (Presbyter-
ian) – there is a tradition of the public singing of metrical
psalms on Sundays, but no tradition of a daily service
centred on psalmody. It is worth noting also that older
Protestant hymnwriters such as Isaac Watts modelled their
hymns on psalms and thus maintained in Nonconformity
the tradition of singing psalms.

CHANGING SCENE

The period since the Second World War has witnessed an
increasing hesitation on the part of both Catholics and
Protestants to use the psalms as the basis for meditation
and prayer (public or private). This is reflected not only in
the way that psalmody is sometimes cut to the very
minimum in worship but also in such measures as the
placing of square brackets around those verses which seem
to be unacceptable for Christian worship (see e.g. the use
of brackets in the psalter in the *Alternative Service Book*
(1980) of the Church of England). Then there are booklets

available which provide simple paraphrases of some of the more easily appreciated psalms to be used instead of the more formal translations in the prayerbooks.

Obviously there are various reasons why the Psalter has lost its popularity with and hold upon the majority of clergy and laity – not to mention monks and nuns. In the Church of England, for example, the tradition of using and singing the psalms in church schools has virtually disappeared and with it has gone the general demise of the church choir to lead in the chanting of psalms. Further, not only does psalmody have to compete with modern hymns, it also requires some effort to appreciate! We must be aware that it does not yield its spiritual results immediately to a generation raised on instant coffee and easy credit.

Probably the most important reason is that (generally speaking) Christians have lost the art of praying the psalms both with Christ and as members of his Body. No longer do we find it easy to pray the psalms (in Calvin's memorable phrase) "through the mouth of Christ". Put another way Christians now are taught/tend to read the psalms as ancient prayers belonging to a long-gone religious context, usually associated with the Temple in Jerusalem. Thus while some seem to be reasonably relevant or transferable into the contemporary situation most appear to be on a first – and maybe second – reading remote.

That which is primarily responsible for this comparatively new situation is the influence of what is called the higher criticism (in contrast to the lower criticism) of the Bible. Now we can claim to know a lot about the origin of psalmody, the type of poetry reflected in it, the contexts in which the psalms were written, their use in the Temple, and the ways they have been edited before reaching their final form as we have it in the Psalter. All this information can be most interesting and, rightly used, liturgically and spiritually helpful. Particular features have been the rediscovery of the dramatic choreography implicit in some psalms (see e.g. a modern commentary on Psalm 118), the greater understanding of the repetitive nature of Hebrew poetry called parallelism (see e.g. the parallel lines in Psalm 6, verses 1–2) and a more secure foundation for a messianic reading of the Psalms because of the connexion of many of them with the monarchy.

CONTRAST

The dramatic shift in the interpretation of the Psalter which has occurred in the Church in modern times may be illustrated by looking at the approach found in two books on the psalms, both by Baptists. The modern book is *The Psalms: introduced and newly translated for today's readers* by Harry Mowvley (Collins, 1989) and the older book is from the famous Victorian preacher, C.H. Spurgeon entitled *The Treasury of David* (1872). The former has very little to say about the Christian interpretation of the psalms and is primarily concerned with explaining the original meaning and use of the psalms in Judah/Israel. The latter shows some interest in the original use of each psalm but gives pride of place to the Christian interpretation of it.

The difference can be illustrated by noticing the approach of each to Psalm 24. Mowvley's primary concern is to help the reader picture a procession of worshippers carring the Ark of the Covenant up the hill of Zion towards the Temple as a recollection of re-enactment of king David bringing the Ark to Jerusalem (2 Samuel 6). Only at the end and very briefly does he mention its use by

Christians as referring to the Ascension of Jesus into heaven. In contrast, while Spurgeon notes the original context his aim is to see how the words address Christians concerning purity of heart and of ascending with their Lord Jesus into heaven.

Spurgeon's commentary includes quotations from a range of earlier writers, including such Church Fathers as Tertullian and Augustine. There is a valuable collection of comments by these two and other commentators from the first fifteen centuries of the Church's history in J.M. Neale, *A Commentary on the Psalms: from Primitive and Medieval Writers* (1869). Anyone who reads these two books – or in fact any commentary on the Psalms by a Catholic or Protestant teacher before the mid-nineteenth century – will find that the major concern is always the Christian interpretation. In other words the Psalter is seen as the prayerbook of Jesus, incarnate, crucified and exalted, and of his Body, the Church, and it is read, understood and prayed in the light of God's redeeming activity in Jesus. Centuries ago the Christian meaning of a psalm was collected in a prayer (a Collect) in order to offer it to God and to remember it. Reading these Collects today is a quick and rewarding way into this traditional Christian way of praying the psalms. (See further B. Magee, *The Psalm Collects*, Dublin, 1978.)

Such an approach seems strange, odd, even offensive and unacceptable to many Christians today. Because we like to get back to things as they are (e.g. to expose the original oak beams of the country cottage) and know why things are as they are, we find it difficult to accept that a later interpretation can be as valid – in fact more valid – than the first or an earlier one. Yet we must admit that when Jesus Christ used these prayers he used them as his own contemporary prayers. On the Cross, as he expired bearing the weight of the guilt of human sin, he prayed in the words of Psalm 22 – "My God, My God, why have you forsaken me . . .". And when the apostles used the psalms they read them in the light of Jesus, the Messiah – his crucifixion, resurrection, exaltation and sending of the Spirit to create the people of the new covenant, his Body. This is why there are so many quotations and citations from the psalms in the books of the New Testament.

When the way Jesus and the apostles used the Psalter is understood it is easy to see why the Church accepted the Psalms not merely as the hymnbook of Israel/Judaism but as the prayerbook of Jesus, Messiah, Lord and Head of the Church. Thus it was entirely appropriate and altogether according to the "mind of Christ" (1 Cor. 2:16) for the Church to read and pray the psalms both with Jesus, the great high priest, and in union with him as the Head of the Body. So it is not at all surprising that the psalms eventually came to be used daily both in corporate worship and private prayers. Generations of Christians used sentences and phrases from the psalms as their own prayers as well as modelling their own compositions upon the style of the psalms.

Regrettably, as we have noted, this way of using the psalms has virtually disappeared in large parts of western Christianity. This is even the case where a tradition is maintained of singing/saying/praying the psalms in a regular pattern. Now their use is usually justified only on the (sound and well-founded) basis that certain psalms accurately express various moods of human nature – fear, joy, depression, anger and so on – and others express joy, praise, thanks and relief. Certainly many psalms provide a mirror or window into the human soul. And, of course, there are some psalms which have so entered our religious heritage that we cannot easily forget them, e.g. Psalm 23, "The Lord is my Shepherd".

A WAY FORWARD

It would seem that until there is a deeply-held conviction by a sufficient number within the Church that we ought to recover the Psalter as our primary prayerbook little will be done to help Christians actually pray all the psalms with and in the Lord Jesus. Individuals who feel the inner urge to pray the psalms in the traditional manner will need to learn the principles of interpretation (typology) used by the early Fathers and their successors and then integrate this into their own deepening experience of Christ in his Body. The very act of seeking to pray the psalms with Jesus and in his Body will be in itself both a meditation and a prayer. Within this approach the modern way of studying the psalms will be seen as most useful, but belonging to preparatory study, helpful yet preliminary and – in the last analysis – not absolutely necessary.

To begin to meditate upon and pray the psalms in the traditional way most people will find that the use of an older commentary (along with a "conservative" modern one – e.g. that by Derek Kidner, IVP, 1973) will be the best way forward. There are the oft-used comments of Augustine of Hippo in his *Enarrations upon the Psalms* as well as the books by Spurgeon and Neale mentioned above. To these may be added the compact commentary of David Dickson, the seventeenth-century Scottish divine. Anyone embarking on this method of reading, meditating upon and praying the psalms will find that it takes not a little time. However, after several months it will be

170

possible to be less dependent upon the commentary since the Christ-centred method of interpretation will have been caught. Yet another way forward is for a meditation group to meet once a week in order, with the help of one of the books we have mentioned, to attempt to recapture the authentic Christian interpretation of the Psalter. In such a group, apart from the periods of guided silent meditation, there will probably be need for times of sharing and discussion in order to grasp the patristic method of reading the Psalter. With this method there is, of course, the danger of thinking that we are looking into the depths of Scripture when we are only looking at the reflection of our own face. This is why using good commentaries and gaining a sound knowledge of the Creed are important both as good preliminaries and constant checks.

Those who use a written service (e.g. the shortened forms of Morning and Evening Prayer in both the Catholic and Anglican Prayer Books) will already have psalms chosen for them for each day. Perhaps their best way forward is to prepare for the praying of the psalm before beginning the office so that in the office it can be prayed with and in Christ. However, if that is not possible then it can be prayed in the office and then immediately afterwards its riches of meaning discovered in brief (formative reading) meditation. (Having said this, I would not want to devalue the daily use of the psalms without meditation, a discipline which has been called "stream prayer", in contrast to the method of meditating/praying each psalm which has been called "the prayer of careful concentration".)

Obviously the benefits of this discipline will hardly be immediate. It is the constant day by day, month by month, and year by year reading and praying the psalms with the mind of Christ which creates not merely a veneer but rather a solid foundation of spiritual life and insight in the Christian soul. One well-known modern Christian who found this to be true was Dietrich Bonhoeffer; but in his case it took the pressure of the Nazi oppression in Germany to make him turn to the psalms looking for a word from God through them. What he did find is recorded in *Meditating upon the Word* (Cowley Publications, Cambridge, Mass., 1986). Yet another modern Christian, whose popularity does not wane and who had to struggle to be able to pray the psalms before the found great comfort in them is the late C.S. Lewis. His book, *Reflections on the Psalms* (Collins, 1970) may be for many still the best introduction to the Psalter as a book of poems which are prayers. I have also found Tremper Longman, *How to read the Psalms*, (IVP, 1988) useful.

Perhaps we all ought both to feel a bond with Christian spirituality of the past and to see the pressure of secularization as sufficiently challenging to make us seek to pray the psalms authentically with and in Jesus as members of his Body.

17
Doing Theology
by Meditation

It is difficult today to find serious books on theology which are in the form of written meditations. Certainly parts of Karl Barth's *Church Dogmatics* read like meditations and several of the books of Hans Urs Von Balthasar are unashamedly in the form of meditations – e.g. his *The Threefold Garland* (1982). However, these are the exception rather than the rule.

Of course if we take meditation to mean pondering and considering which includes speculating then a much larger number of modern books in theology could be called meditation. That is, they are the expression of serious and discursive thinking about a religious subject. However, if we take meditation to mean the prayerful consideration of God's self-revelation with a view to worshipping, loving and serving him then we limit what may be called theological meditation. In fact such meditation may be said to arise from the position summarized by Augustine and Anselm as *credo ut intelligam* (I believe in order that I may understand). That is, while meditation is the work of the intellect seeking to understand what God has done and said it is the work of an intellect which belongs to a person who is intent on trusting and loving God, and who cares only to glorify God.

THE CONTEXT

Perhaps the reason why so few apparently "do theology" through prayerful meditation is to be sought in the intellectual ethos and atmosphere of the modern western university. Today the theologian is very conscious that she/ he has to sit, as it were, facing the world and academic colleagues for the exercises of thinking and writing: kneeling in prayer is for the chapel not for the study and seminar room. Thus systematic theology is often based on the reverse of the Augustinian or Anselmian formula – i.e. I seek to understand in order that I may have grounds for belief. This is not to say that university-based theologians are not Christian believers – some are and some are not. It is to say that to be able to pursue their careers they need to work within the generally accepted context of the secular university. (We have already faced this general problem in chapter 15 with reference to Biblical studies.)

To do even a part of one's theology by meditation is to make a decision concerning priorities. If the primary task of the theologian within the Church is seen to be that of paying attention to what God has revealed of himself in order to be able to respond and guide the modern Church in its response, then she/he will of necessity be a meditating theologian! Now a meditating theologian need not only produce theology as written meditations: in fact it is possible that she/he will produce no published written meditations. However, the general output of such a theologian in lecturing and writing will have the hallmark of the meditator – one who has believingly and prayerfully and humbly paid the closest attention to God in his self-revelation. This will be seen both in the style and the content of writing/lecturing/tutoring, be it in the field of

174

dogmatic/systematic theology, apologetics, philosophical theology or any other branch.

Of course, being a meditating theologian is no guarantee of truth for in the work of theological statement there is no guarantee of final truth, only of approximation to the Truth which is Jesus, the Christ. The point is that whatever the intellectual gifts of the theologian and however devoted he is to "seeking the face of God" there is no way that he/she can ever do other than seek to approximate to Truth. However, the theologian is called not only to think clearly but also to be holy and mature in the Faith and to be so he will of necessity be one who meditates and prays.

ANSELM

It will be useful to look back over to the centuries to see how Anselm understood the place of meditation in the doing of theology. For him meditating upon God's truth is set in the context of having leisure for God and withdrawing in order to encounter him. This movement into a specific consciousness of the presence of God is described in oft-quoted words from chapter one of his *Proslogion*, which take the form of a soliloquy:

> Come now, little man,
> turn aside for a while from your daily employment,
> escape for a moment from the tumult of your thoughts.
> Put aside your weighty cares,
> let your burdensome distractions wait,
> free yourself awhile for God
> and rest awhile in him.
> Enter the inner chamber of your soul,
> shut out everything except God

175

and that which can help you in seeking him,
and when you have shut the door, seek him.
Now my whole heart, say to God,
    'I seek your face,
    Lord it is your face I seek'.

From soliloquy he moves to colloquy as he has a dialogue
with God as he seeks him with all his soul – mind, heart
and will. In fact it is in his dialogue/colloquy, described in
the Proslogion that he actually provides the famous "argument" for the existence of God known as the "ontological
argument" (God is that than which a greater cannot be
thought). I suspect that few who study this argument in
philosophy classes realize the context in which it is found –
prayer to God!

The whole spirit of his approach is well stated in the
closing lines of chapter one:

Lord, I am not trying to make my way to your height,
for my understanding is in no way equal to that,
but I do desire to understand a little of your truth
    which my heart already believes and loves.
I do not seek to understand so that I may believe,
    but I believe so that I may understand;
        and what is more,
I believe that unless I do believe I shall not understand.

This is a classic statement of the patristic theme of "Faith
in search of understanding".

To do theology in such a way not only requires that the
meditator has been endowed by God with a powerful
intellect but also that the meditator is spiritually/morally
prepared for this holy search. Anselm insisted that there
must not only be withdrawal but also self-knowledge and

compunction of heart. To know oneself aright is to know God's estimate of the human person as a guilty sinner, deserving of wrath and condemnation, but granted pardon and peace through the shed blood of Jesus. Such knowledge leads to the piercing of the heart, to godly sorrow, to the desire to know God and be with him always. As the psalmist put it, "in your light [O God] we see light". To seek God on the basis of his self-revelation to mankind is not like attempting to solve an intellectual puzzle or to find a way through a maze. It is to be submitted to him as Lord and King, to be repentant before him as Judge, to be desirous of his love as Father, and to long for his presence as Spirit. This is to seek God primarily for God's sake since he as Creator and Judge alone is truly worthy of being sought for his own sake.

The true ethos of theological meditation is marvellously captured in the closing prayer of the *Proslogion*, of which the last part is as follows:

> God of truth,
>   I ask that I may receive,
>   so that my joy may be full.
>   Meanwhile let my mind meditate on it,
> let my tongue speak of it,
> let my heart love it,
> let my mouth preach it,
> let my soul hunger for it,
> my flesh thirst for it,
> and my whole being desire it.
> until I enter into the joy of my Lord,
> who is God one and triune, blessed forever. Amen.

There is to be no barrier between mind (thinking) heart (feeling) and will (doing) in the loving of God for God's sake. Though the theologian has a special duty in the realm of studying the Faith and its implications he has a general duty, common to all Christians, to imitate Jesus in the loving of God and the neighbour.

LIGHT FROM MARTIN LUTHER?

In a little essay entitled "A right way to study theology" he proposed three rules – *oratio*, *meditatio*, and *tentatio* – which he claimed to find set forth in Psalm 119 (in Preface to Vol. 1. of the Wittenberg edition of his *Works* of 1539: in *W.A.* vol. 50, pp. 658–661.) Working from his strongly held view that the contents of Holy Scripture (which teach the doctrine of eternal life) make foolishness of the wisdom of all other books he urged the pastor or student to act in this way: "Kneel down in your study and pray to God in true humility and earnestness, that through his dear Son he may grant you his Holy Spirit to enlighten, guide and give you understanding". This is *oratio* – prayer.

The next step is *meditatio* and he advised as follows: "You should meditate not only in your heart but also outwardly, repeating and comparing the actual, literal words in the book, reading and re-reading them with careful attention and thought as to what the Holy Spirit means by them". Further he cautioned the meditator: "Guard against being satiated or thinking that when you have read, heard, or said it once you have understood it fully – for this will never make an excellent theologian".

The final – and perhaps surprising step to modern ears – is *tentatio*, trial. Luther believed passionately that the true theologian would confront the devil in his ways and works and be severely tempted by him. The trial, or the proving, of faith was Luther claimed "the touchstone that teaches you not only to know and understand but also to experience how right, how sweet, how lovely, how mighty, how comforting is God's Word, the wisdom above all wisdom".

There is usually more than a glimmer of truth in everything Luther wrote and here he surely has put his finger on something quite important. A theologian, to be genuinely Christian, must be a person who prays, who meditates, and who seeks to fight with and for Christ against the world, the flesh and the devil!

VIABLE TODAY?

While it may not be realistic to encourage academic theologians to attempt to produce theological works which are the result of prayerful intellectual meditation, it is, I think, realistic to encourage students of theology in Christian seminaries and colleges to practise the art of doing theology by meditation. By so doing there would be the possibility of uniting head and heart, classroom and chapel, academia and church, time and eternity. For it may be true to claim that a theology which cannot be converted into prayer to the Father in the name of Jesus Christ is hardly a genuine Christian theology at all.

What is advisable for the student is surely also possible for the working clergyman as well as for certain of the laity who have aptitude and time. For theological meditation is a form of mental prayer which exercises the muscles of the mind in the highest calling of the mind – to love God and to know him. Many congregations and parishes would surely benefit if their clergy made space and time regularly to reflect prayerfully on the great doctrines of the Faith as these are presented in Scripture and summarized in Creeds

and Confessions. This meditation could well arise normally through the daily reading and meditating on Scripture
and the conscientious keeping of the ecclesiastical year
with its great themes of Incarnation, Reconciliation/Atone-
ment, Resurrection/Ascension, Holy Spirit, the Holy Trinity and so on. Anyone who is called regularly to preach
the Word of God ought to see such meditation as a joyful
necessity, for faith is in search of understanding in order to
love God the more.

18
Becoming Contemplative

Not only the word meditation but also the word contemplation bears variety of meanings today. Ignatius of Loyola used contemplation of the imaginative seeing of Jesus – e.g. picturing him being baptized in the Jordan or being forced to carry the beam of his cross. In contrast, seventeenth century Protestant writers such as Richard Baxter often used contemplation simply as a synonym for meditation – and this usage continues in Protestant piety. To complicate the picture still further, not a few, especially in the modern retreat movement, use the expression "contemplative prayer" for what (by traditional standards) is only the very beginnings of the life of prayer; and others, inside and outside this movement, use the expresion to describe the silence and inner harmony they achieve by the use of eastern techniques.

Perhaps it will be helpful for us briefly to set out the most widely accepted description of the life and grades of prayer in the Roman Catholic Church today, so that against this structure we can set our own presentation of meditation and hopefully see the spiritual reality to which various (technical) words and phrases point. This list is based on the teaching of St Teresa of Avila, and I follow the general exposition of Jordan Aumann in his *Spiritual Theology* (Sheed & Ward, 1986). I shall make my comments within square brackets so that they are seen to be separate from the summary.

1. Vocal Prayer

This is the prayer that is spoken in public worship, in prayer meetings, and by an individual alone. The most widely used vocal prayer is the "Our Father . . ." taught by our Lord. For vocal prayer to be truly prayer addressed to the Father through the Son and by the Holy Spirit it needs to fulfil two requirements. In the first place awareness and attention – thinking of the content of the words said; and, in the second place, devotion, offered from a believing, humble and loving heart to God our Father.

2. Meditation

This is "a reasoned application of the mind to some supernatural truth in order to penetrate its meaning, love it and carry it into practice with the assistance of divine grace". It is not speculative study of a truth from the Bible or Creed but a pondering in faith of that truth with the aim of loving God and the neighbour: thus it includes the making of resolutions to put into practice what has been understood and felt. [Strictly defined meditation is here only discursive, that is, it does not include the prayer which naturally arises from the heart which is moved by the truth seen by the intellect – cf. the testimony of George Müller above, chapter fourteen. Protestants usually include within their understanding of meditation the prayer which arises from the considering, pondering and reflecting upon either the actual text of Scripture or truths based upon Scripture.]

3. Affective Prayer

Normally discursive meditation or spiritual reading [of

Bible or of spiritual classics like the Imitation of Christ by Thomas à Kempis] stimulate the will and thus make possible the practice of prayer which arises in the affections – in the desiring, longing for, loving, hoping for, believing in, fearing and reverencing God and wanting to see his will done on earth as it is in heaven. "Psychologically, it provides a delightful respite from the dry labour of discursive meditation." Thus affective prayer ought naturally to follow on from and even intersperse the act of discursive meditation. [Protestant writers include affective prayer within their general definition of meditation and do not see it as a separate category. Further, there is a very rich literature in Protestantism on the exercise of the affections – perhaps the greatest book is Jonathan Edwards, *The Religious Affections*. Further, it is probably useful to say that some methods of meditation do seem to be more naturally related to affective prayer. I think especially of the method developed by Dom Chautard OCR in his classic, *The Soul of the Apostolate* (trans. J.A. Moran, Dublin, 1957). It is summarized in four Latin expressions – *Video* (I see); *Sitio* (I thirst); *Volo* (I wish) and *Volo Tecum* (I wish with Thee).]

4. Prayer of Simplicity

This expression derives from Jacques Bossuet (d.1704) and was called "acquired recollection" by St Teresa. It has also been called "the prayer of acquired contemplation". Whatever it be called it is the simple vision of faith, the gazing adoringly and lovingly upon God in one or another of his attributes or perfections. It is a spiritual seeing by faith and in love of the glory of God in the face of Jesus Christ our Lord. The affections have been unified and with the mind are attracted to God and are held steadily gazing upon him for a longer or shorter period. Affective prayer can and ought to be a step toward this more intense form of prayer, which may but does not necessarily follow it. A further point needs to be made. The gazing upon God can bring both joy and sorrow, happiness and pain, because to see God in his glory is also to see our own sins (cf. the vision of Isaiah, in Is.6). [Again, this experience of prayer is well recorded in Protestant diaries and accounts of meditation and prayer; however, it is treated as part of the mature practice of meditation – see the testimony of Edwards and Brainerd in chapter fourteen above.]

5. Contemplative Prayer

Here we have crossed over from what is called ascetical prayer to what is called mysticism, mystical prayer, and contemplation [This is an area which Protestants have been hesitant to explore because they have been suspicious of the vocabulary and concepts used – see especially Friedrich Heiler, *Das Gebet* (Eng. trans., *Prayer*, 1932). Heiler distinguishes between mysticism and prophetic piety and tends to see the latter as more authentically Christian then mysticism. However, there have been Protestants who have described their mystical experiences – e.g. Sadhu Sundar Singh – and there are others who have had similar experience of God in prayer to that of St Teresa and St John of the Cross but who have used a more biblically-based language to describe it. The evidence for this may be seen in Simon Chan, *Meditation, Puritan-style* (Cambridge University Press, 1990). I have often tried to show that the Puritan teaching that meditating upon the glorified Jesus Christ who is in heaven is the highest form of meditation is perhaps something of a divine equivalent to contemplation in classic Roman Catholic exposition – see my *Longing for Heaven*, MacMillan, New York, 1989.]

Contemplation points to the experience of knowing God and is accompanied by delight, admiration and enrapture. It is only possible through the help and leading of the Holy Spirit, and it only occurs within those who are truly seeking to be holy and perfect as disciples of Jesus. In this form of prayer the soul is more passive than active because it is made still by the felt presence of God and the sight of God who is holy and glorious. There are ever deepening forms of contemplation and they are described as the Prayer of Quiet, the Prayer of Union, the Prayer of Conforming Union, and the Prayer of Transforming Union. God calls all his children into this form of prayer but since only a few genuinely seek perfection only a few enter into this experience of contemplative prayer.

*

There is obviously a need for those who have explored the depths and heights of meditation/prayer in the different Christian traditions to have more dialogue in order both to learn from each other and to see how and where different vocabulary points not to different experience but to the same form of the knowing of God through Jesus our Lord. Further, there is a great need to study carefully the claims often made today that mysticism in eastern religions is much the same as or identical with authentic Christian mysticism.

Epilogue

We have come to the end of our presentation of meditation as a basic way of waiting upon the Lord. Beginning from Psalm 123 in the Prologue, we have noticed through the eighteen chapters that true Christians, like genuine servants, wait upon and look to the Lord, their God, reverentially – in holy awe, obediently – doing his commandments, attentively – with a loving gaze, continuously – by day and night, expectantly – with a ready heart, submissively – as to an all-wise Father, and imploringly – hoping for mercy.

To close our study we turn to one of the most moving and sublimest confessions of faith found in Holy Scripture, that in Isaiah 40:27–31. To appreciate this and how it relates to the theme of waiting upon the Lord, we need to recall the historical situation in which it first was heard as the words of God. The Jews had known long years of captivity in Babylon under foreign, pagan rule and this had embittered them and filled them with self-pity – so much so that they accused their covenant God of having totally ignored their plight (v.27). To counter this accusation from his elect people, God responded through the prophet in these words:

> Do you not know?
>   Have you not heard?
> The LORD is the everlasting God,
>   the Creator of the ends of the earth.
> He will not grow tired or weary,

and his understanding no-one can
fathom.
He gives stength to the weary
   and increases the power of the weak.
Even youths grow tired and weary,
   and young men stumble and fall;
but those who hope in the LORD
   will renew their strength.
They will soar on wings like eagles;
   they will run and not grow weary,
   they will walk and not be faint.

God not only has power but he also gives power. While the strong and stalwart fall exhausted on life's journey, the faint and weary (made strong and stalwart through waiting upon God) receive strength to complete their journey. To all who wait upon him the Lord imparts new strength: their failing strength is exchanged for God's unfailing strength.

It is a big mistake to see an anti-climax in v.31 – from flying majestically like an eagle, to running and finally to walking. This is a right description of the life of faith, the life on which the Christian meditator has embarked. There will be times when the waiting upon the Lord will bring such experience of the presence, guidance and power of God that living for Christ will be like soaring in the sky or running fast over the hills.

However, most of the time being a disciple of Jesus will be the steadfast walking by faith through whatever providential circumstances God sends in our direction. So the test of faith comes to us not when flying or running but when merely plodding along. It is in the monotony of daily life that the discipline of meditation helps the Christian live by faith.